Psychic Pets

The Secret Life of Animals

JOSEPH EDWARD WYLDER

BONANZA BOOKS
New York

This 1989 edition is published by Bonanza Books, distributed by Crown Publishers, Inc., 225 Park Avenue South, New York, New York 10003, by arrangement with Esther Mitgang.

Printed and bound in the United States of America

Library of Congress Cataloging-in-Publication Data

Wylder, Joseph Edward.
Psychic pets : the secret life of animals / Joseph E. Wylder.
p.   cm.
Reprint. Originally published: New York : Stonehill Pub. Co., 1978.
Includes bibliographical references (p.
ISBN 0-517-69265-1
1. Extrasensory perception in animals.   2. Pets.   3. Animal behavior.   I. Title.
[QL785.3.W95   1989]
133.8—dc20   89-18216   CIP

Book design by Francesca Belanger

h   g   f   e   d   c   b   a

Contents

On the Making of a Psychic Pet

Anyone who has lived closely with his or her pet has a basic grasp of what promises to be a crucial phase in human intellectual history. While pet owners do not generally view themselves as members of a group engaged in important scientific research, the fact is that the reports of those who have observed their animals may very well be the basis for some of the most startling revelations in the study of uncanny animal behavior.

There are many reasons why people decide to own pets—to ease their own loneliness, to protect property, or for a purpose as practical as ridding a house or barn of mice. But much to some owner's surprise, they soon realize that they have entered into a very special relationship with a creature whose powers far exceed anything which the owner had been reared to expect. Pets, originally purchased as aristocratic creatures of display to be paraded in local shows often end up in incalculably different roles—as confidants, peers, teachers.

Those who have already experienced the mysterious power of the animal kingdom can pinpoint the exact moment when they first realized that their pet was operating on a level far different from—and vastly superior to—that which the pet had first been given credit for. A cat leaps onto the telephone table and makes worried feline sounds just before the phone rings with an important message; or a dog suddenly, without warning, goes through a radical behavior change, pacing and whining, and the owner has no idea why; an hour later, a loved one comes knocking at the door and the dog, finally, curls up in contented sleep. One close friend first glimpsed the psychic power of animals in a tragic way. Her pet canary, Lucy, began to chatter wildly—something the ordinarily placid and heedless bird never did—at the sound of a bicycle being pedaled up the front walk. The cause of the commotion? A Western Union messenger was bringing news of my friend's sister's death— the sister who had given her the canary a few months earlier.

Pet owners have an abundance of stories like these. Some of these stories demonstrate the profound instinctual powers of animals and their highly developed senses of smell and hearing. Yet others cannot be satisfactorily explained by studying the animal's biological nature, and take us beyond the five senses, beyond instinct, and into the realm of the psychic. Even those tales which demonstrate the complex (and magnificent) biological nature of animals are important and deeply instructive to humans. Yet our real education begins when we learn that our pets have powers of which we had never dreamed—powers which often surpass human abilities!

The power of precognition. The power of ESP. The power of telepathy. And the power to experience a love so pure and deep that it can only be called cosmic. These are but some of the unique abilities your pet can display...if you learn how to tune into them.

How is it that our pets can read our thoughts? How do they sense our private emotions, even when we ourselves may not be fully aware of them? Many who have relationships with animals ask themselves these questions but because the answers may take them beyond the well-worn path of accepted knowledge, the questions are left unanswered.

In observing pets and their human companions, as well as through studying the literature dealing with the animal sixth sense, it has been found that those animals with the most highly developed sixth sense are usually those who are most deeply loved by their owners. If not nurtured, the sixth sense in animals will atrophy, or at least remain hidden from human observation. Though a particularly intelligent pet will develop itself and its sixth sense under most circumstances, the most remarkable communications between animal and human need a large measure of human cooperation—a cooperation based on respect for and belief in the animal's innate powers.

Can every pet be a psychic pet? Just as there are intellectual and emotional limits in humans, there are limits beyond which many a pet cannot pass. In fact, some animal companions are even dull, due to such factors as over-breeding, in-breeding, biochemical misfortunes, or psychological traumas. There are also certain *limits* characteristic of the different species. Yet despite all of the innate qualities which can affect a pet's psychic ability, none is quite so important as the human's ability to communicate with the animal. Even the least psychic of animals can, if properly approached, teach us a great deal about the sixth sense.

Nowhere is the complexity and psychic rigorousness of non-human social life better illustrated than in the kingdom of the honey bee. One of the most cogent descriptions of the intricate world of the bee appeared in *The First New England Catalogue*. The author, Eugene Keyarts, brilliantly captures the intense social life of this common insect:

In a colony, the queen is capable of laying 2,000 eggs every day. She has the ability to control the sex of each of these eggs and determines whether an egg shall hatch as a worker (female) or drone (male). There is no such thing as a "queen bee egg." It is impossible for a queen to reproduce one of her own kind. The creation or conception of a queen bee is solely the decision of worker bees.

When an old queen dies or abdicates, potential queens are selected by the workers. Any worker egg or larva, not more than three days old, may be chosen for the dubious honor. Incredible as it may seem, a worker egg left to develop without interference develops the complex organism that is a worker bee. She nurses the larvae, makes wax and comb, keeps the hive clean and guards against intruders, then spends the last days of her brief life ... foraging in the fields for pollen and nectar. The worker bee performs all those chores necessary for the welfare of the colony, with one execption, that of egg-laying. But give the same worker larva a little more "Lebensraum", keep it on a strict diet of "royal jelly" and it becomes an equally complex organism—that of the queen bee—following an entirely different route of development and accomplishment. One notable change is the queen's life span, which may extend from six to eight years in comparison to the worker's short six weeks.

A queen bee does not gain her high office by descending from a royal line or by divine right. She and several other worker eggs are nominated candidates by groups of their peers throughout the hive. Those selected are given special attention and fed royal jelly, which actually transforms and prepares them for their royal duties.

When the workers have chosen an egg or larva, harbinger of a queen that may eventually reign over them, they tear down the walls of the cell in which the candidate lies and start building a queen cell around her. When completed, a queen cell, made of wax and usually attached to the side of the comb, resembles a peanut shell in size, shape, and color. As the princess advances through the larval stage, she is fed by nurse bees. The candidates feed so copiously, they actually float in a sea of royal jelly inside their cell. Royal jelly is a secretion produced by glands in the nurse bee's head. Sixteen days after the egg is laid, the fully matured princess gnaws her way out of her cell to declare her sovereignty.

Once free of her confining quarters, she sounds a high-pitched challenge to any other pretenders who may be ready to contest her right to be queen. Customarily, the workers nominate more than one candidate to strive for the high office of ruling monarch and build several queen cells at about the same time. The first princess to emerge rushes to those queen cells from which come answers to her challenge; tearing the cells to shreds, she stings her competitors to death. These assasinations continue until all her rivals have been vanquished, after which she takes a well-earned rest, then swiftly walks about on an inspection tour of her domain. She is not yet accepted by her sisters, they do not crowd around her, she must first prove herself by returning from a successful nuptial flight.

Four to ten days after her victory over her rivals, the surviving princess prepares for her wedding flight. On a bright, sunshiny day she takes wing, to mate, high in the air, with the fastest flying drone of those who pursue her. He couples with her in mid-air, dying in the act, actually exploding and depositing millions of spermatozoa in a pouch within the bride's body. The queen seldom mates more than once in her lifetime, thereafter becoming both mother and father to all the eggs she may lay . . .

Arriving home, she is immediately surrounded by her royal attendants who take care of her every need from now on. They wash, clean, massage, comb, feed her.

The new queen starts laying within 48 hours after mating. She inspects each cell carefully to see that it is properly cleaned and polished. Having satisfied herself that a cell is ready to receive an egg, she stradles the cell, inserts her long slender abdomen into it and leaves a single egg. Even during the few seconds required to lay an egg, the queen's royal ladies-in-waiting groom and feed her.

The endless round of egg laying is repeated over and over for the rest of the queen's life . . . A queen may lay millions of eggs in her lifetime. She controls the sex of each egg by touching it with a speck of the father's sperm to produce a sterile female worker or withholding the sperm to produce a drone. But she does not decide when or how many eggs to lay. This decision is made by the nurses. When there is sufficient pollen being harvested to feed the larvae, the nurses stuff the queen with royal jelly and she continues to lay at top speed.

When the pollen supply falls off, the nurses restrict the queen's intake of royal jelly and she immediately slows down or stops her egg laying activity.

All animals are constantly communicating with one another through the silent language. Clearly and without question, all animals on earth have the power to communicate silently with one another. This power is shared by even plant and vegetable life, fish of the sea, the tiniest organisms squiggling beneath the microscope. At one time in human history, it seems certain, we shared that same power. We have, however, gradually lost and forgotten it as our conscious, verbal means of communication became more and more dominant. In that way, the discovery of our pet's psychic powers is a rediscovery of our own.

A pet may not always be able to understand or interpret all that it perceives in its owner, but in all cases the psychic realm is modulating and informing your pet's behavior. Whether you choose to or not, you are sending psychic waves which most animals can automatically receive. That is why some animals seem to be such precise and instinctual judges of human character, why some people seem to have such immediate friendships with animals while others find themselves avoided or mistrusted. We have all seen examples of this and have, to one degree or another, explained it by acknowledging certain hidden perceptual powers in animals. Yet even those who recognize and trust the perceptions of their animals often fail to take the next step.

Those moments of extraordinary perception we see in animals are connected to a full and complete system of understanding which is always in operation. Once we can recognize this body of psychic knowledge, this arsenal of psychic skills in our animals, we can enter into a wholly unique and intense relationship with our pets based on their—and our own—psychic powers, and allow our pets to teach us a silent language we once knew, but have lost over the ages.

PART ONE

Psychic Dogs

Telepathic Dogs

Perhaps no other single animal has inspired such rhapsodies of affection and nostalgia as the dog. Even pet owners who have never entertained the idea of psychic power in animals find themselves loving their canine companions with a loyalty and fervor often bordering on the religious. Some who scoff at the very idea of psychic power can be heard to remark that *their* dog in fact does seem to sense unspoken thoughts and feelings. Humans act out all types of impulses and desires through their dogs. Some compensate for lives of frustration by severely disciplining and even terrorizing their dogs. Some attempt to make up for the lack of human contact by treating their dogs as if they were four-legged people—dressing them in costumes, feeding them specially prepared meals, and in general abusing the dog's *animal* nature. In fact, the extraordinary receptiveity of the dog makes it a target for abuse—its forgiving nature is often mistaken for insensitivity or slavishness, and its very special consciousness is recognized, at best, as an "almost-human" intelligence.

Dogs are perhaps unique among the domesticated animals because they have *chosen* domestication, forsaking the life of the wild for a life with humans. While this theory is controversial, the world-renowned animal behaviorist Konrad Lorenz makes a convincing case for it in his remarkable *Man Meets Dog*. Whatever the origins of the relationship between canines and humans, one thing is certain: dogs love nothing better than to be in communication with their "masters," whether this communication is aural, physical, emotional, or psychic. Just by a mere pat on the head, a human can elicit an incredible range of reactions from a dog—tail-wagging, eye-widening, nuzzling, licking. And each of these reactions—far too often taken for granted and overlooked by humans—has a specific meaning. Dogs have many ways of communicating with each other and with you through body movements. Each small gesture has a highly specific meaning.

For example, when your dog furrows its brow, cocks its ears and tilts its head slightly, you can be sure it is concentrating with every sense, including its psychic scanners, so it may interpret a sound, a scent, or a movement. Your dog's barking, howling, and whining can be broken down into pitch, length and curve of sound waves, and duration. Through careful study of these differentials, we can begin to discern a canine language. These various canine sounds are certainly understood by dogs, and inside the species play the role of spoken words. Of course, within the complex and intensely social world of dogs, smell plays a major role in communication. No dog will greet another without a thorough sniffing over. In this way, friendly dogs are positively identified. Male dogs in particular are continually marking off the area they consider their territory by urinating on trees, posts, and even tall blades of grass. And rubbing into his or her coat the odor of a recent or decaying kill is to your dog what dressing in the finest, most prestigious *haute couture* is to a lady. In the case of your dog, the smell of decaying matter boasts of his or her being a good hunter, and this commands attention and admiration in other canines.

Yet even with the astonishingly acute olfactory senses and his highly developed auditory sense, your dog's most critical channel of communication goes far beyond the physical. A canine depends on extrasensory perception—ESP—not only to communicate with members of his own species but with humans. Your dog's telepathy usually works on a low level, or cruising speed. If it is not acknowledged and developed by us—through our love and respect—it will most likely remain at just the level needed for everyday living, geared more toward communication with other dogs than with humans. In fact, most dogs, because of their owner's lack of knowledge and imagination, don't have the stimulation needed to develop their psychic abilities to their fullest. Yet once a pet owner opens the channels for equal give and take of thoughts and feelings, the results can be truly astounding. Your dog will continue to be lovable, playful, entertaining, and loyal. But an incredible new dimension will have been added to your relationship that will not only deepen your appreciation of your dog's innate powers—it will deepen your understanding of all of life.

One of the most detailed and classic accounts of canine ESP is reported by J. Allen Boone in his widely discussed *Kinship With All Life*. In that book, Boone describes his uncanny relationship with an ex-Army dog turned movie dog named Strongheart. Strongheart, a full-bred German Shepherd, was, through his Army experiences and his work in films, highly trained and accustomed to constant and detailed communication with humans. Strongheart was fortunate to have a trainer named Larry Trimble whose interest in the dog exceeded the merely practical. Trimble didn't want just a highly disciplined dog who would perform on command. His intention was to find a canine with the highest aptitude for thinking, a gentle nature, and experience in using the sixth sense. In Strongheart, Trimble found all these.

One day, Trimble had to leave for an extended business trip and he asked Boone if he might leave Strongheart in his care. Boone readily agreed because, like so many other movie fans, he admired Strongheart. He thought it would be fascinating to spend time with such a well-trained animal. Boone was given detailed instructions regarding Strongheart's care—bathing, feeding, grooming—and all that one might expect to hear from a doting dog owner. But what Boone did *not* expect to hear was the admonition that he must never talk down to Strongheart or show disrespect of any kind. And that—

most importantly!—Boone was to read something "worthwhile" to Strongheart every day.

Boone accepted these instructions without fuss. He looped the collar and lead onto Strongheart's neck and went home with the dog. Upon reaching the house, Strongheart nudged Boone aside, took the door-handle in his mouth and turned and opened it. Strongheart then bounded into the house, opening and closing doors, inspecting closets, checking each room and sniffing almost every object in sight. Then he returned to Boone for further instructions.

This was only the beginning. From that moment on, Boone knew he was not dealing with an ordinary dog; though it was not until later that Boone realized he was destined to learn great things from Strongheart.

That night, Boone and Strongheart lay down in bed for a good night's rest. But Strongheart continually leaped up at the noises of the night and each attentive, protective jolt sent Boone tumbling out of bed onto the floor. After a few such tumbles, Boone reproached Strongheart in no uncertain terms. Either he would calm down, Boone said, or he, Strongheart, would have to find some other place to sleep. Strongheart took in all of this, standing in his alert, military manner. Then an astonishing thing happened. Strongheart took hold of the sleeve of Boone's pajamas and led him to the french doors toward which he'd been leaping after each noise. Then the dog released Boone, walked up to the doors, and pulled aside the curtains. Looking from the windows to Boone and back again, Strongheart was able to explain the whole reason for his posture in bed and for his constant vigilance. He had explained in a language as clear as words what he needed, and the reason behind it: in order to be a good protector, Strongheart had to sleep facing the french doors. And so Boone, with Strongheart's assistance, turned the bed around so they could both sleep facing the doors.

"For the first time," writes Boone, "I was actually conscious of being in rational correspondence with an animal. With the dog's patient and guiding help, we had been able to express our individual states of mind to each other. Yes, it was as though Strongheart had been able to write him long, highly anecdotal letters. I realized how little I knew about the mental capacities of a dog, and his ability to express those capacities in a practical way."

But Boone's education did not end there. Strongheart continued to astound his new companion. For instance, the dog demanded that bedtime and the time of rising be exactly the same each day, and he would tolerate no variation. Yet, Strongheart knew how to be considerate as well. He knew not to interrupt Boone when he was writing. If Strongheart wanted some amusement, he would open the closet door, choose a toy that caught his fancy and close the closet again. When he was finished playing with the toy outside he would come back into the house—on his own—and open the closet, replace the toy in exactly the spot from which it had been taken, close the door again, and settle down.

These and other actions were clearly the marks of a highly— perhaps phenomenally—intelligent animal whose thought processes seemed closely linked to the logical progressions of human thought. Yet as impressive as his intellect was, this was not the truest mark of Strongheart's capacities.

In his relationship with Boone, Strongheart seemed to sense a kinship which allowed him to open up freely, as he had with his true master Larry Trimble. As man and dog grew closer each day, Strongheart initiated the next stage of their relationship, the ascent to the dog's truer mode of communication—ESP. Boone had had little experience with this realm of contavg, but for Strongheart it was entirely natural.

Boone first discovered Strongheart's exceptional abilities one day when he decided that he'd rather not spend the day at home, working at his desk. What he would much rather do, Boone thought, was spend the afternoon with Strongheart, walking in the hills. When Boone's mind was firmly fixed on not working that day, Strongheart who'd been outside playing, burst open the backdoor, ran to Boone, licked his hand, and proceeded, in separate trips, to bring from the bedroom Boone's sweater, blue jeans, boots, and walking stick.

Boone had not said a word, nor betrayed his decision with a gesture, yet no more than a few seconds had separated his decision to take a walk and Strongheart's exuberant entrance. Clearly, some other form of communication had been at work here.

Boone had been getting a glimpse of what so many other dog owners experience—canine ESP. Sometimes this ESP takes the form it did in the case just described; sometimes it is shown by the dog's sensing danger, or death. Some people try to classify—and so dismiss—this astoundingly keen canine sensibility as a kind of instinct. But what is *instinct*?

Strongheart and Boone were soon inseparable. They walked, played, took late afternoon naps, and Boone read aloud to him. The writer came to accept and expect that Strongheart could "read" his thoughts. Strongheart used his precognition to live in harmony with Boone, and certainly to witness this was a marvel. Yet after a certain point, Boone could not help but be dissatisfied. The psychic communication was still just one way. The burden of it rested solely on Strongheart. If the relationship were to reach its full potential, Boone would have to gain the ability to *receive*, as well as to send, telepathic communications. He dearly wanted to establish two-way communication, and Strongheart was willing and able to teach him how.

Strongheart began Boone's initiation with simple things, such as staring long and intently into Boone's eyes and forcing him to stare back. It was an incredible experience for Boone—quite like being pulled bodily from one dimension into the next. Boone sensed what was happening to him, that his entire world and all of his assumptions were being re-made. His courage was such that he refused to panic, refused to turn away from psychic truths which were being rapidly unveiled before him. Strongheart continued to peer deeply into his eyes, forcing Boone's mind to open and release the psychic energies which all of us have, but which fail to come into play because we neither recognize nor nurture them.

As time went on, Boone began to feel within his mind the

stirrings of some previously unknown, unfelt force.

Boone was a good and brave student. He concentrated on Strongheart's every move, every emotion, and he worked hard at establishing the open psychic passages through which free, telepathic communication is possible. All the while, he continued to be Strongheart's caretaker, doing all that was involved for his teacher that the dog couldn't do for himself.

By breaking down his own ego and by transcending the habits of his intellect, Boone, with Strongheart's constant, loving assistance, was finally able to establish free-flowing psychic communication with his canine friend. Often, they sat upon a cliff and together silently gazed into the starry night. At such moments, Boone was utterly attuned to the dog's thoughts. He could hear and interpret the universal language, the silent, wordless communication which at one time existed between all living things and which is, when it is finally recaptured, immediately understood.

From the moment their psychic channels were fully open to one another, Boone and Strongheart were virtually inseparable. Indeed, Boone hardly expected such profound companionship from his human friends! The writer reports that he and Strongheart sat together for hours, exchanging thoughts and feelings—silently, simply, harmoniously. Just as a wanderer, coming by chance into a hitherto unvisited part of the forest, may be struck by the sensation that all living things there—the trees, ferns, clover, birds—have been interrupted in an everlasting conversation, so would an unwitting intruder feel on coming upon Boone and Strongheart. Theirs truly was the unspoken language which preceded the language of symbols and words.

Throughout *Psychic Pets*, we will have occasion to discuss many marvelous animals. We will describe how their behavior serves to re-educate us as to their real nature. We will meet animals with mathematical ability, animals who predict weather, animals with clairvoyant powers. We will discuss how the silent language of animals operates within the animal kingdom and how the gap is bridged that this tongue can be understood—and learned—by humans.

Strongheart is perhaps not altogether unusual, and the story of his profound communication with Boone is not the most startling story we will recount in these pages. But the story of Strongheart and Boone is, to me, one of the most touching in the annals of psychic animal lore. It is the story of a highly conscious animal who sensed in a human being the possibility for a profound relationship. It is the story of how one man's trust in an animal enabled him to break through the barrier of habit and intellect and make use of the psychological powers and senses which had remained dormant within him.

The German Ambassadors: Talking Dogs

A student of animal behavior cannot help but be struck by the abundance of Germanic names listed in the literature; German Science has a long history of observation and reflectiveness regarding the ways of animals. While a dog who can understand and speak human language and who can also exhibit considerable mathematical skill could conceivably appear anywhere on earth, it is, I think, fitting that two of the most famous and carefully studied logical canines were bred in Germany.

The first dog we will discuss is named Rolf. Rolf, an Airedale—a breed famed even in traditionalist circles for its alertness and intelligence—was owned by a woman known in the literature of the extraordinary as Frau Moekel.

One evening, Frau Moekel was helping her young daughter with her homework, in a scene characteristic of a humdrum evening at home. The child, bathed and fed, was working on arithmatic, while the mother, watchful and stern, stood by. At one point in the evening, the child hit a stumbling block. She could not, no matter how she tried, figure out the answer to a simple sum: 122 plus 2. Mother Moekel, with a severity and harshness that many today might find shocking, grew impatient with her daughter. As a way of reproving the flustered child, she turned to Rolf, who was watching, sprawled under the desk.

"Rolf," said Frau Moekel," tell this silly child what the answer is!"

Rolf was fully aware of what was taking place between mother and child. It may even occur to some that he should simply have leaped on Frau Moekel and bitten her. But Rolf had a far more subtle way of dealing with the problem of his mistress' severity. Getting up from under the desk, he sat attentively at Frau Moekel's side. She asked Rolf if he knew the answer. to a simple problem. "How much is two plus two?"

To Frau Moekel's enormous surprise—not to say utter shock!— Rolf answered with four distinct taps of his paw. Startled, she asked him next what five plus five was. Sure enough, Rolf tapped his paw ten times.

During that first session, Rolf was doing sums correctly, understanding numbers up to one hundred. He seemed to enjoy himself, and Frau Moekel's little girl, let us assume, was relieved of her mother's attention. After all, why waste time browbeating a dull girl when there's a dog apt at arithmetic?

Frau Moekel, the wife of a respected lawyer, began to devote herself to Rolf's education. Teaching the dog became her daily occupation. In a short while, Rolf was extracting the square roots of two and three. From this complicated mathematical feat, he went on to verbal dexterity. He allowed Frau Moekel to teach him to recognize letters and to understand the words they formed. Finally, her attitude changing from one of curiosity to one of awe, Frau Moekel began to want to communicate more directly with Rolf. She was, clearly, far too ego-bound and traditional in her responses to be reached in the way J. Allen Boone was reached by Strongheart, but Rolf was determined to reach her by any means possible. So he learned to make paw signals for *ja* and *nein*. Then he learned to represent every letter in the alphabet in this same manner.

It did not take long for articles to be featured about Rolf in German newspapers and magazines. Put on public display, the dog and Frau Moekel traveled all over the land. Rolf did complicated sums and had weighty conversations with his mistress before scientists, animal lovers, and curiosity seekers. Rolf would demonstrate his musical knowledge by tapping out the number of tones struck in a chord, and showed that he had somewhat of a green paw by identifying each flower in a bouquet presented to him.

As Rolf was studied more closely, people began to learn that his responses were really quite complicated. Surely, those who came in contact with this sharp-witted representative of his species were never able to look at a dog with condescension again. For instance, Rolf was capable of pithy retorts. When Professor Mackenzie of Genoa asked Rolf the meaning of "autumn," Rolf replied, "Time for apples." In an excellent account given years later by Vincent and Margaret Gaddis, we also learn that Rolf had a roguish sense of humor. The occasion was an examination by an eminent French psychologist named Monsieur Edmond Duchatel, who visited Rolf accompanied by an elderly and very proper lady who served as his secretary. During the testing, the woman was invited to ask Rolf a question. Probably she was sensitive enough to realize that Rolf had been asked to do enough and it was high time for someone to offer to do something for him. She asked, "Rolf, is there anything you would like me to do for you?" Rolf's answer: "Wag your tail!"

Rolf's abilities to communicate with humans were passed on to a female he sired, an Airedale terrier named Lola. The scientific community was anxious to know and study an heiress of the famous Rolf. But as attempts were made to develop the dog's special powers it became apparent that Lola was unreachable; her commonplace nature was blamed on her dam, an unexceptional dog named Jela. Lola was passed from household to household, for many were eager to possess a psychic dog—yet no one, it seemed, had any success with her. Even Frau Moekel could teach Lola only a very basic conversational tool: to tap her paw twice if she meant "yes" and three times for "no." Beyond that point, Lola's understanding and abilities to communicate could not be expanded.

She was turned over to a woman named Henny Kindermann,

who, through her relationship to Lola, went on to write one of the most extraordinary and thrilling documents in the literature of animal behavior.

Frau Kindermann had faith in Lola, and Lola sensed this. Yet in order to communicate successfully with Lola, Henny Kindermann had to undergo certain changes in her character. As she tells us, "I felt that I had become calmer and more self-possessed, and this, too, reacted on the dog...I also attempted to make her understand that she would be able to help other dogs—in fact help all dear animals, if she was industrious in showing people how much a dog could do."

Since Henny Kindermann wanted to teach Lola to do difficult sums, a shorthand or, so to say, a short-paw was invented. If the question was how much is seven multipled by four, Lola could answer with two taps of the left paw and eight taps of the right paw, rather than twenty-eight taps of one paw. If Lola wanted to denote one hundred she would tap her left paw ten times.

Like her father, Lola had a good head for figures. She allowed herself to be trained in such a way that her knowledge was readily apparent to humans. (It is, we have learned, one thing for an animal to possess skills and wisdom, but quite another matter for the animal to display these qualities to people. Many more animals are potential wizards than we imagine! Those who do come to the public eye represent only the tip of the iceberg.) She could do rather tricky problems, such as three times three plus ten minus five.

Then, in Frau Kindermann's words, "My thoughts now turned to the matter of spelling. A total of figures from 1 to 40 would suffice in order to express all the sounds, while the same degree of comprehension of my spoken words was all I required." Frau Kindermann, whose experiences with Lola developed her into a rather meticulous recorder of data, has done us the service of making her Lola Language Chart, based on German, available to us:

a	e	i	o	u	au	ei
4	5	6	7	8	9	10
b&p	d&t	f&v	s&k	ch	ü	h
14	15	16	17	20	21	24
l	m	n	r	s	w	z
25	26	27	34	35	36	37
		ja	nein	g		
		2	3	23		

With the invention of this canine alphabet, Lola's studies were arranged so she could work on language mornings and mathematics afternoons. Then, again in Henny Kindermann's own words, "As soon as she had mastered the entire alphabet I proceeded to combine the letters into words. I said: 'Lola, now listen You are going to learn to spell. You must rap out a word made of the letters you have learnt; now *Wald* [wood or forest] is W.A.L.D.,' and I accentuated each letter very distinctly. 'How many letters are there in this word?' I asked, and the answer was four. 'Good,' I said. 'What is the first letter?' She tapped 36 times in reply for 'W.' 'And the next?' Four taps for 'A.'" In this methodical way, Lola's vocabulary grew by leaps and bounds. In fact, Lola's use of Kindermann's code became so expert that it soon exceeded her teacher's ability to record it.

One day, Frau Kindermann asked Lola—as way of an experiment—"What is this?" while touching the dog's nose. Lola was uncertain but then replied with three paw-taps, which meant *"nein"* or "no." Kindermann said, "Lola, this is your *nose*; tap the word for nose." Lola tapped out 27-4-35-5, which spelled *Nase*, the German for nose. Kindermann immediately touched Lola's eye and asked her what that was. With no difficulty or hesitation, Lola tapped out 9 and 23, which according to the code was *aug*, a slight misspelling of the German for eye, which is *"auge."*

The next stage in Lola's education—or was it Henny Kindermann who was *really* being educated to understand the incredible hidden powers of animals?—was to learn how to read. Henny wrote the number 1 on a sheet of paper, and then placed one dot beneath the number. Then a 2, with two dots beneath that, and so on up to 10.

As Henny tells us, "I then held this sheet a few inches from her eyes and, pointing to each, said, '*One* dot looks like 1,' et cetera. At the start, this gave her a great deal of trouble...I helped her and then set the sheet up near the place where she usually lay, assuming that in the course of the day her eye would be bound to rest on it so frequently that she would probably retain the impression the next day. And something of this kind must have happened.

"On the following morning, after having gone through the explanation once more, putting the sheet aside, I wrote the dog symbols at random on another sheet of paper. She actually 'spotted' them all—with the exception of 7, but a comparison of the two sheets enabled her to put this right, too. There could be no doubt that she had really mastered her lesson, for the replies were tapped out with absolute certainty."

In a very few days, Lola was solving *written* arithmetic problems. To Henny's surprise, Lola hardly spent any time studying the problem on the sheet. The dog would merely glance down and then "the gaze was withdrawn, so to speak, as it is in the eyes of a person engaged in the process of thinking." In moments, Lola would come up with the correct solution to the problem.

From there, it was not very difficult to teach Lola to read letters and words. Using her phonetic knowledge of the alphabet and combining it with her recently acquired ability to read numbers, Kindermann wrote out:

a	e	i	o	u	au	ei
4	5	6	7	8	9	10

and so on. She gave a short explanation to Lola, left the sheet on the floor, trusting the dog to do her studying on her own. (Canine students are apparently different from human ones!) Sure enough, the next morning Lola was ready for her lessons. She'd been given the entire alphabet to learn and had some difficulty keeping it all straight. Yet by the second day, she was reading nearly perfectly. Whenever she had difficulty deciphering a word she would, without Henny's assistance, consult the original sheet she'd used to learn from.

Lola, like her father Rolf, chose to communicate with humans in the way they would be most receptive to and most likely to understand—that is, in human terms, as a student of language and numbers.

Lola and Rolf, of course, are not the only dogs on record who have chosen to enter into rational discourse with human beings. A famous American example of this phenomenon was a beagle mix named Chris, who was known far and wide as Chris the Mathematical Mongrel. Chris, who lived in Rhode Island was a well-known celebrity in the late Nineteen Fifties, appearing in night clubs and on television and allowing himself to be studied by scientists and professors from places such as the Rhode Island College of Education and Duke University. Chris could subtract, multiply, divide, and do square and cube roots. Like Lola and Rolf, he tapped his answers out on the arm of the questioner.

Another American canine genius was a Llewellyn setter known as Jim the Wonder Dog, who was studied carefully by professors and scientists in his home state of Missouri. Jim could pick out trees by name, and in a famous demonstration before a gathering of students and faculty at the University of Missouri, Jim obeyed commands to pick out a particular girl in the crowd, a man with a mustache, various makes of automobiles, and a particular license plate number. To make his performance even more remarkable, Jim responded to directions spoken in English, Italian, French, and German.

Whenever one of these prodigious dogs comes into public view, we can assume two things. First, that it is not only one of many animals with that skill, but one who has gotten the attention of the press; and, second, that there are many, many other animals who could do as much if someone asked it of them. Indeed, Lola did not volunteer her incredible mathematical and reading abilities; if she had not been related to a famous learning dog, no one would have dreamed she'd be capable of acquiring the things she eventually mastered.

Lola's abilities became more and more complex, more and more impressive. Though she was being encouraged to relate to people in a purely intellectual way—which is not, we have learned, the deepest animal faculty—Lola did manage to stretch the imagination of the humans around her by giving them messages from the psychic realm.

For instance, one day she disappeared for a long while. When her mistress asked her where she'd been she answered, "In the woods." When asked what she had been doing in the woods, Lola confessed she had gone to "marry" a male admirer. She went on to cite how many puppies would be in her litter, and she was later proven absolutely correct. Both Lola and her father Rolf were adept at predicting the weather as well. Rolf warned those around him of the Mannheim earthquake which struck in 1912; Lola regularly gave weather forecasts, three, four, and five days in advance—predicting rain, sun, or snow with more accuracy than our two-legged TV forecasters.

As Lola became more accustomed to using the language of humans, she managed to teach those around her some very important lessons regarding what we can only call "consciousness." In other words, she passed through the stage of merely answering questions with direct information and began to give a real, startling indication of how her thought processes worked.

She demonstrated a sense of self by one day spontaneously referring to herself as "I" rather than as Lola, as she had always done until then. Asked one day if she would like to be a human being, Lola tapped a quick, emphatic "No." When asked why not, Lola answered that people worked too hard! Then she was asked by Henny Kindermann, "Do you belong to me, Lola?" Lola answered, very energetically, "No!" "To whom do you belong then?" Lola answered, "Myself."

One day, curiously, Lola confessed to telling a lie! And a few days after that, she complained to her mistress that she was getting too little nourishment from her food. She began to express her own sense of the abstract, as well. Asked to perform some mathematical feat one day, she declined. Asked why she refused to do it, Lola said, "I have a reason without knowing it." Then she began to tremble and said she felt cold. Asked why she was alive—for her demonstrations of consciousness and insight had excited those around her—Lola answered, "It is all the same to me. I like living."

Lola and Frau Kindermann now seemed to have gone through a difficult period. The cause of this, as Henny Kindermann herself finally understood, was that Lola wanted their relationship to rise above the intellectual plane and progress to the psychic. After urging Henny in this direction and meeting with little success, Lola lodged her complaint one day by suddenly addressing Henny as *"Sie,"* which is the German formal way of saying "you," whereas *"Du"* or "thou," is informally used between friends. Shocked, Henny asked Lola why she used *"Sie,"* and Lola answered that it was because Henny was "strange." Her teacher knew that something was seriously amiss, and did her best to change her character so Lola might be happier. Lola's oft repeated request was that Henny not ask her to do so exclusively the purely intellectual exercises. In this way, she urged her mistress to step over the line and join her in a more cosmic means of communication. Yet how could this be done? What was the step necessary? When Henny asked Lola for an answer, this is what she told her mistress: "Show constancy in your love for me."

Has anyone known a dog who has not made, in one way or another, that very same request?

THREE

Secret Life

I n order to throw into relief some of the astonishing, true stories of pets and psychic phenomena, perhaps it would be well to discuss for a moment a few of the common, everyday ways in which our animals conduct themselves.

As any close observer of animal behavior can tell you, animal society is rather rigidly codified. With its customs, elaborate greetings, stylized signs of respect and domination, intense regard for territory and seniority, it reminds one of what human society used to be—in the time, say, of Elizabethan England. Some social scientists—among them, Richard Sennet, in his book, *The Fall of Public Man*—have observed that evolution away from formal, ritualized behavior in human society has meant a falling off of intimacy and meaning. If you've been fortunate enough to be able to observe your pet relating naturally and freely to other animals, then you've had a glimpse of some of the prodigious everyday social powers that all animals possess.

An animal's ability to be at one with his environment is, aside from any spiritual meaning we may assign to it, essential to the animal's survival. In even the simplest animal societies, intricate systems of identification and communication exist. A mother buffalo has no trouble whatsoever in picking out her offspring even in the midst of a stampeding herd.

In species whose social order and survival is built on the principle of permanent monogamy (such as the butterfly fish, pigeons, jackals, whales, parrots, and marmosets), elaborate and inflexible systems of calls, flight patterns, and gestures serve to identify the mate in ways that can—and must—never err. In some species, the act of reproduction is connected to a cosmic sense of the total environment. The common buzzard, for example, will allow as many members of its nestlings to survive as can be supported by that year's supply of mice.

Nowhere is the complexity and psychic rigorousness of non-human social life better illustrated than in the kingdom of the honey bee. One of the most cogent descriptions of the intricate world of the bee was printed in *The First New England Catalogue*. The author, Eugene Keyarts, brilliantly captures the intense social life of this common insect:

"In a colony, the queen is capable of laying 2,000 eggs every day. She has the ability to control the sex of each of these eggs and determines whether an egg shall hatch as a worker (female) or drone (male). There is no such thing as a 'queen bee egg.' It is impossible for a queen to reproduce one of her own kind. The creation or conception of a queen bee is solely the decision of worker bees.

"When an old queen dies or abdicates, potential queens are selected by the workers. Any worker egg or larva, not more than three days old, may be chosen for the dubious honor. Incredible as it may seem, a worker egg left to develop without interference develops the complex organism that is a worker bee. She nurses the larvae, makes wax and comb, keeps the hive clean and guards against intruders, then spends the last days of her brief life ... foraging in the fields for pollen and nectar. The worker bee performs all the chores necessary for the welfare of the colony, with one exception, that of egg-laying. But give the same worker larva a little more 'Lebensraum,' keep it on a strict diet of royal jelly and it becomes an equally complex organism—that of the queen bee—following an entirely different route of development and accomplishment. One notable change is the queen's life span, which may extend from six to eight years in comparison to the worker's short six weeks.

"A queen bee does not gain her high office by descending from a royal line or by divine right. She and several other worker eggs are nominated candidates by groups of their peers throughout the hive. Those selected are given special attention and fed royal jelly, which actually transforms and prepares them for their royal duties.

"When the workers have chosen an egg or larva, harbinger of a queen that may eventually reign over them, they tear down the walls of the cell in which the candidate lies and start building a queen cell around her. When completed, the queen cell, made of wax and usually attached to the side of the comb, resembles a peanut shell in size, shape, and color. As the princess advances through the larval stage, she is fed by nurse bees. The candidates feed so copiously they actually float in a sea of royal jelly inside their cell. Royal jelly is a secretion produced by glands in the nurse bee's head. Sixteen days after the egg is laid, the fully matured princess gnaws her way out of her cell to declare her sovereignty.

"Once free of her confining quarters, she sounds a high-pitched challenge to any pretenders who may be ready to contest her right to be queen. Customarily, the workers nominate more than one candidate to strive for the high office of ruling monarch and build several queen cells at about the same time. The first princess to emerge rushes to those queen cells from which come answers to her challenge; tearing the cells to shreds, she stings her competitors to death. These assassinations continue until all her rivals have been vanquished, after which she takes a well-earned rest, then swiftly walks about on an inspection tour of her domain. She is not yet accepted by her sisters, they do not crowd around her, she must first prove herself by returning from a successful nuptial flight.

"Four to ten days after her victory over her rivals, the surviving princess prepares for her wedding flight. On a bright, sunshiny day she takes wing, to mate high in the air with the fastest flying drone of those who pursue her. He couples with her in mid-air, dying in the act, actually exploding and depositing millions of spermatozoa in a pouch within the bride's body. The queen seldom mates more than once in her lifetime, therafter becoming both mother and father to all the eggs she may lay...

"Arriving home, she is immediately surrounded by her royal attendants who take care of her every need from now on. They wash, clean, massage, comb, feed her.

"The new queen starts laying within forty-eight hours after mating. She inspects each cell carefully to see that it is properly cleaned and polished. Having satisfied herself that a cell is ready to receive an egg, she straddles the cell, inserts her long slender abdomen into it and leaves a single egg. Even during the few seconds required to lay an egg, the queen's royal ladies-in-waiting groom and feed her.

"The endless round of egg laying is repeated over and over for the rest of the queen's life... A queen may lay millions of eggs in her lifetime. She controls the sex of each egg by touching it with a speck of the father's sperm to produce a sterile female worker or withholding the sperm to produce a drone. But she does not decide when or how many eggs to lay. This decision is made by the nurses. When there is sufficient pollen being harvested to feed the larvae, the nurses stuff the queen with royal jelly and she continues to lay at top speed.

"When the pollen supply falls off, the nurses restrict the queen's intake of royal jelly and she immediately slows down or stops her egg-laying activity."

Interestingly enough, with the current renaissance of interest in human biological origins, more and more people have taken up bee-keeping as a hobby. Although my early training has left me with a slight fear of bees and I do not keep them myself, many of my neighbors have become confirmed apiarists. The obvious benefit of this pastime, of course, is the honey harvest; but in every case I've come across, the material benefit of bee-keeping soon takes a back seat to the great educational and psychological value gained from contact with these complex, ritualized creatures.

We are, newspapers and TV tell us, living in the Age of Communication. But what stranger and more accurate mode of communication is there than the constant, symbolic, and unconscious communication between members of the hive? With an instantaneousness far exceeding that of the manmade electronic "global village," the social life of the hive is a perfect example of how perfect communication insures the survival of the species. (And if humankind should ever become extinct, what greater single cause will there be than a lack of communication?)

Humans seem to have relinquished their more psychic modes of communication in favor of audible, logical language. Of course, the development of speech was a necessary step as we evolved into the creatures who would do the present-day work of humankind. And it would be sheer foolishness to wish that we had never learned language—that we had remained mute, communicating only through gazes and ESP.

But a law of nature seems to be that of the trade-off. We gain certain attributes at the expense of others. The first creatures to crawl out of the sea eventually sacrificed their ability to breathe beneath the water so they might develop the ability to live on land. Likewise, we have sacrificed many of our intuitive qualities as we have developed our logical minds—and as we go further along the path of technological sophistication we stand to drift even further from our ancient powers of telepathy and precognition. We are losing as well, our sense of oneness with nature.

Only a few of nature's most privileged creations keep one set of skills as they develop the next: The platypus, for example, is equally at home on land or at sea. Those few humans who are known far and wide as "psychic" seem to be to be like the platypus, living in two worlds at once: the world of our everyday rational thought, and the more elemental world of our psychic past. We refer to such people as having a "sixth sense," as if the ability to hear the unspoken or see the invisible were an extra sense, grafted on the others. But it is just as plausible to believe that the so-called sixth sense is the *first* sense—our original means of perception. The psychics have then simply managed to hold on to it, despite thousands of years of evolutionary drift.

One of the great privileges of being able to form friendships with animals is that a careful, loving relationship with them teaches us (or *reminds* us) of our own psychic pasts, our psychic potentialities. Even if we are with animals who do not show us their truly mystical natures, who do not initiate us into a relationship as profound as the one between Strongheart and Boone, there is virtually no limit to what we can learn from observing our pets and taking them very seriously.

All animals have very complex relationships with their environment, and possess a variety of mechanisms for dealing with the world at large, with humans, with potential prey, and with members of their own species. The dog, for example, has a very wide repertory of facial and bodily expressions, without which he would be quite helpless.

The body language of your dog is fairly straightforward and easy to interpret—though some dogs are more subtle than others, or lack a tail to wag, or jo not have enough facial hair to manipulate for different expressions. Within the canine social structure, communication includes expressions of emotion mostly transmitted by way of the tail and the head. This topic has been widely and competently investigated by such researchers as Charles Darwin, in his *The Expression of the Emotion in Men and Animals*, and Eberhard Trumler, a Konrad Lorenz disciple, in his detailed book entitled *Your Dog and You*.

When one dog meets another, there occurs an immediate ritual of greeting. Though these greetings seem to contain much subtle and detailed information, the "bottom line" appears to be a question of dominance and submissiveness. Always critical are the circumstances of these meetings—which to many dogs are the very stuff of life. These encounters are as crucial as a social life is to many humans—and include such factors as who is on whose territory, who smells of a recent hunting expedition, etc. Within moments, the dogs will distinguish their particular roles, and will communicate their acceptance of the rules of canine society through various kinds of body language: the subordinate of the two will relax his ears, stand cautiously with his tail lowered and wagging very slowly; or, if he feels truly bested and threatened, he may even roll onto his back and show his belly. The "top dog" will prance, soldier-like, with ears erect and pointed forward, and an intent look in his eyes. His tail will be up and wagging rigidly like a baton.

After the dogs have identified and ranked themselves, they are ready to proceed with their visit on the terms set. If they are males they will urinate on a nearby tree (or lamppost, or whatever is available) to indicate territory. The dominant of the two will explore confidently, while the subordinate follows cautiously at a distance. The right to be the first to smell things is heavily imprinted in dogs. A puppy who lives with his sire is not allowed to sniff at any thing—even a leaf—without his father's permission. If the pup breaks the rule, he is thoroughly disciplined. This may seem rather harsh, but it is based on a safety factor, since the father has no confidence in the pup's ability to discriminate between the benign and the dangerous.

The meeting we have just described is a very general one, on foreign territory. Dog watchers will recognize that the description lacks detail because in the space of a minute's meeting most dogs will display a dozen social signals, each one rich in meaning. The dog's world is based on instant recognition of the state of mind and intentions of every other dog he meets. Just as humans, suddenly finding themselves thrust together in an elevator, size one another up by interpreting visual clues, so do dogs. The difference is that dogs are never wrong. They absolutely *know*.

When we meet a dog we should be able to understand quite a lot about it by reading its body language—the dog, to be sure, knows a lot about us in that way! For example, if you meet a strange dog in the process of doing the rounds of its neighborhood, the dog may greet you cheerfully. Its tail will wag freely and its facial expression will be relaxed. Chances are the dog will give you a quick sniff before going about the business of the day—which no doubt will consist of a few specific visits and in numerable markings-off of territory. There is no reason to be concerned for your safety when confronting an animal whose body language speaks of relaxation and good intentions—for even though many animals, and particularly dogs, are clever enough to lie, the language of the body is always truthful. You can depend on such signs as wide eyes, ears that are relaxed or bent slightly sideways, and a slack mouth that gives the dog a kind of grinning expression.

On the other hand, you may meet a shy dog, or what is sometimes called a "fear-biter." Dogs, because they are such intensely social animals, often have rather marked personality defects. The body language of a shy dog is more subtle and confusing than that of a confident, friendly animal. The dog will appear submissive, or perhaps lost and frightened. The eyes will dart, the ears will lie flat, and the tail will be carried low, moving back and forth like a military mine-sweeper. To some, such an animal may appear sweet and endearing—but the shy dog is also giving very clever indications of its instability, and its tendency to lash out because of fear. While a cowering dog, with its tense muscles and hunched shoulders, may appear to be so defeated as to pose no threat, it is just this sort of animal that can cause an unpleasant situation.

A crucial part of a dog's social life is expressed through the voice. Dogs, of course, with their phenomenally sensitive ears, are very much attuned to acoustic clues. As Eberhard Trumler points out, "Every dog has his own individual voice."

Yet the voice is more than a mode of identification. For those who pay attention, the different sounds a dog makes can and will make constitute a canine language which we should learn to understand—just as we expect our dogs to understand such human commands as "Sit," "Stay," and "Come." Most often, a dog's attempt to speak to us will be accompanied by body language.

A typical example is described by Trumler: "Many dogs wishing to induce their masters to play with them adopt the typical attitude which dogs use between themselves: they crouch down in front, rear ends in the air with wagging tail, head and eyes directed on the object of their challenge; this is an unmistakable posture of invitation. Since Master is often busy with other matters and does not notice, (or does not want to notice), our Fido now has recourse to his voice—he uses his yelp, which signifies submission, in order to attract attention."

Understanding the exact meaning of your pet's various sounds comes only after many hours of concentration and communication. If you choose to interpret the throaty sounds of your cat as just so much meaningless noise, then you can never expect to penetrate the secret world of animals. If you react to your dog's—or your canary's or horse's—sounds as if they had no meaning, you will remain excluded from their world.

There was a book published recently by Jhan Robbins, former president of the Society of Magazine Writers and Pulitzer Prize nominee. He has long been fascinated by animal language, and his book *Your Pet's Secret Language* is available for anyone interested in a better understanding of his pet.* In his book, Robbins lists one hundred words which, according to Dr. John Paul Scott of Bowling Green University, make up the easily attained vocabulary of a dog. The interesting thing about this list is that even those who don't believe their dogs understand human language find that, sure enough, their dogs *do* recognize the words on the list. These include such staples as "bad," "ball," "no," "out," "sit," and "good," as well as the more exotic "cookie," "friend," and "garden."

Robbins also lists some fairly typical sounds made by your dog in its attempt to communicate with you. Most of them are accompanied by body language: for example, with the sound Robbins describes as "Don't tease me," your dog will lie on the floor, several feet away from you. His ears will be down and his tail tucked between his legs. Opening and shutting his mouth, he will make a loud clicking sound which Robbins describes as sounding like "Clark Kent, Clark Kent."

Another, far happier sound, is one which Robbins describes as "I am in total agreement." For this, your dog will cock his ears, tilt his face to the left and make several short, clipped barks. Conversely, when the dog is not in total agreement, the ears will be down and the face will be tilted toward the right, and the barks will be of a noticeably higher pitch. Some of the dog's communication will be wholly spoken.

Such things as a growl at an intruder need no body language accompaniment—no more than would a yelp of pain. The whine emitted by a dog whose master has gone away is unmistakable, and the squeals and high-pitched barks of a dog welcoming a loved one are as recognizable to the dog-fancier as Beethoven's Fifth to the musicologist. During these greetings, many dogs will display a vast vocabulary of sounds, making guttural noises, yips, drawls, yawls, and all manner of sounds. If only more pet owners would pay closer attention to these sounds and learned to assign a specific meaning to each one! In order to do that you must know your individual pet. No guide book or checklist can teach you your pet's language. It is up to you. If you *believe* that these sounds have meaning, if you *want* to know their meaning, you are halfway there. Your pet longs for you to understand *him*, just as your pet deeply desires to understand *you*.

FOUR

Penetrating the Psychic World of Your Pet

Know this: your dog's extrasensory perception is as necessary to his life as his eyes and ears. (The same goes for your cat, by the way, and hundreds of other pets as well.) ESP is developed throughout puppyhood and is used throughout his life. It is an integral part of his identity as a pack animal and it is the keynote of his complex and rich inner world. In the wild, ESP is used as a device in hunting as well as a way of staying in tune with the rest of the pack. In domesticity it is used in coping with the complexities of civilized life and as a way of puzzling out the needs and demands of humans.

In most pets, the sixth sense operates at a kind of cruising speed—keen enough to process the information the dog needs, but not so strong as to be noticeable. The primary reason for this relatively vague use of the sixth sense is, I am firmly convinced, that dog owners' expectations are generally low and/or uninformed. The dog owner who is aware of his or her dog's inner life and *expects* to find it manifested, will actually help to strengthen the dog's psychic potentialities. The dog's psychic nature will be evidenced in direct proportion to his master's belief in it. Those owners who are not inclined to believe that their animals have any special intelligence are, of course, unlikely to be touched by it—unless they are lucky enough to be possessed of pets who are not only psychic but persistent, and determined to educate their masters. Unfortunately, most of our pets aren't so stubborn, and if they are not recognized as being psychic, will not spend much energy proving the point.

Those who have long recognized the psychic power of the canine like to debate which of the breeds has the greatest psychic potential. Mant give the nod to the Airedale; others are convinced that no communication with a dog can match that which is possible with a German Shepherd. Some choose Poodles; others say that because of the economics of dog-breeding, your best bet is to form a psychic bond with a mongrel. I'm completely convinced that the breed (or lack of breed) of your dog makes virtually no difference in terms of opening up the channels of psychic communication. If there is one important variable it is the human being and his or her ability to take the giant intellectual and spiritual step toward recognizing and understanding the dog's complex inner world. Some day, when humans and animals are more freely communicative with one another, we may learn that certain kinds of people have fuller psychic rapports with certain breeds of dogs. But since there is a wide array of personality and alertness within any given breed, it will probably always remain an individual matter. The philosopher Sören Kierkegaard said that every man is an exception. Though the same goes for every woman of course, we ought to remember that it also applies to every animal.

There are some dog owners who like their pets just the way they are—that is, they like to *see* them the way they always have. When a close friend of mine, and a long-time dog owner, saw me developing certain exercises designed to increase psychic communication between my dog and myself, he said, quite seriously, "That's all I'd need! I've got enough problems without a dog with a crystal ball between its ears. I don't want a psychic pet, I just want a *dog*." Well, whatever you might feel about my friend's sentiment (and he's still my friend so *I* forgive him!), the fact of the matter is that whether or not we *like* the idea of psychic pets, we've got them. In other words, it's not a question of making your dog psychic. It's a matter of learning how to recognize an utilize abilities he *already* has.

Your dog's reason for wanting to open the channels of psychic communication with you is really quite simple: he loves you. Just as most dogs will follow their owners from room to room, or will wait patiently at the door or window when their owners are away, so does your dog enjoy having you in his thoughts. Sometimes, your dog's psychic communication with you is a matter of life and death. We will have an opportunity to explore later on a few of the literally thousands of instances when a person has been saved from death by an animal's psychic knowledge.

But it is also often true that a human in psychic contact with a pet can save that pet's life. Jhan Robbins scrupulously reports the case of a woman who, while at work, suddenly thought of her dog and felt an intense wave of fear. She was convinced the dog was in trouble. She immediately dropped what she was doing and rushed home. It's a good thing she did, too. If she had dismissed her dog's psychic call for help, she would have found a dead animal. The dog had entangled himself in a rope and was slowly but surely choking to death. As it turned out he was saved, and quickly recovered from the ordeal. But how many other animals have sent out psychic S.O.S. signals that have gone unheeded?

I have never believed that old adage that tells us you can't teach an old dog new tricks. I have lived with too many different dog companions to believe that. The one thing I am really quite certain of is that of all the things a dog wants—and dog lovers know that list can be mighty long!—right up top is to be in constant communication with his master. By this I don't mean just patting and playing, or even just talking. I mean *telepathic* communication which will enable the dog to be in touch with his master uninterruptedly and, if need be, over great distances.

Begin when your dog is still a puppy—but like any other kind of training, it doesn't do to begin too early. When a puppy is ready to be trained he will let you know through his attitude and body language: his ears will follow sounds and he will locomote himself in a more steady and alert fashion. Because he is beginning to work hard to find his place and role in your household, he will be visibly more attentive, will react to changes in the environment—and you'll begin to find him staring at you, as if trying to figure you out.

When the real training begins, at about your puppy's fourth or fifth month, you have an enormous responsibility: you must develop his innate canine pride. Though the play aspect of the relationship is far from over—and indeed ought never to end—there now comes the time for seriousness. For though dogs are certainly not without a sense of humor, their life, to them is quite serious and your recognition of the seriousness with which they view their impulses and responsibilities is an important step *you* must take if you wish to enter their world. Some of the basic ingredients you must bring to a rich relationship with your dog are respect, affection, patience, open-mindedness, and honesty. There can be no success without these things, and there can be no success if you are inconsistent. Animals have little use for people who are not dependable.

As you begin your dog's training he is carefully noting your attitude. If you are trying to get something across that is somewhat complicated, it's doubly important that you send out all positive signals. Your dog is watching your body and all of your unconscious movements; he is listening carefully to your voice—not only to what you are saying but *how* you're saying it; and he is forming a pretty accurate idea of what you're really thinking.

Often I hear dog owners complain that they've gotten nowhere in training their dogs, even though they've done it "by the book." Of course, they take this to be a failure on the dog's part! But, without exception, I've found that these owners of "stupid" dogs never really believed in their dogs' ability to master difficult tasks. While they were commanding their dogs to do one thing or another they were also thinking, "He'll never get this. He'll never make the connection."

And the poor dog was hearing two things at once: the command and the telepathic discouragement. It's not that the dog then refuses to learn in revenge on his master for having such faithless thoughts, it's just that the conflict is terribly confusing. If you have doubts about the training, or about your dog's ability to learn, the best thing to do is simply to *tell your dog*, so he will understand you and, I guarantee, will forgive you. If this sounds terribly odd, I can only urge you to forget your preconceptions. If you want a relationship with your dog which is out of the ordinary, then you must *do* things that are out of the ordinary.

When training begins it is also time to start experimenting with telepathic communication. But remember: begin slowly. Your dog is still young and has much to learn about himself, about you, and about the world around him. Just as training periods should be rather short, so should sessions of psychic communication. The best way is to combine the two. For instance, while in your training session of the command "Sit," not only should you push his backside gently down, you should reinforce your oral command by *thinking* "Sit"—as often, or even more often, as you say it.

I hasten to add that you must do a little soul-searching before entering this phase. It is essential that you know within yourself what your true expectations are. To enter into psychic communication half-heartedly is to make success unlikely. However, don't think you have to prove to yourself that you have psychic abilities. While some people seem to be more attuned to their psychic nature than others, rest assured that you, like all the creatures of the earth, have powers of cosmic intelligence. It doesn't matter that you don't see ghosts or can't bend keys with your thought waves. Your sixth sense is innate, it is constant, and it is *yours*.

All right. Now, at the beginning of the psychic phase of your dog's training I would recommend your keeping a little notebook— unless you've got a photographic memory. This will help you to know your dog objectively—to separate in your mind what your dog really is, from what you thought he was, or what you'd like him to be. Watch him carefully. Learn his body language. See what excites him. See what he avoids. How do his ears cock when he hears a siren? How about when he hears a blue jay—or when he hears you whistle? Learn to recognize minute differences. Note his actions in and out of doors and note his responses to sunlight, to a full moon, to unexpected movement. Most of all, note his reactions to you, and true to correlate them not only to your explicit actions but to your unspoken moods.

A close friend of mine had a little terrier who was afraid of him—except when my friend was feeling depressed, at which time the usually timid terrier was immediately at his side. When my friend related this story to me I told him his dog was reading his thoughts, and he used this insight to totally improve his relationship with the dog.

This brings us to the all-important second step: you must note, just as carefully, your *own* responses. How do you react when your dog makes a "mistake"? How do you greet the dog? What do you feel about his appearance, his sexuality, his habits? In dealing with these and other questions, you must be honest. There is no point in hedging, or in giving yourself half-answers. Your dog senses the answers to all these questions, and *your* knowing the truth of your feelings will only put you on an equal footing with him.

Next, you should begin talking to your dog. (Once, before I fully learned the value of conversing with pets, I had cause to wonder why so-called "little old ladies" generally had such smart pooches. Well, the answer is that because older people are often very lonely, they spend a lot of time talking to their pets and the pets definitely respond!)

While washing the dishes one evening, you might say to your dog, "I'm washing the dishes." Don't say it as if it were a joke, and for goodness' sake don't say it in a peculiar, unreal voice. Your dog may not understand exactly *what* you've just said but he'll understand that you're saying *something*, and that it is serious, *and* that it was meant for him. And with this knowledge he will extend his own sensibilities, trying to catch on.

Continually point things out to your dog. Tell him out loud that you're mending your pants and even tell him why. Tell him what the weather is, even though he knows. Your dog may respond with a baffled look, or he may wag his tail, or give a few excited yips. He may cock his head, he may even cringe. However, if you've been noting the wide variety of his responses—if you have, in other words, tried to learn his silent language before trying to make psychic contact with him—then you will be able to interpret his reactions with some degree of accuracy.

Read to your dog. Play music (softly!) which he seems to like. Do the things your dog likes to do—it's his world too, you know. Compromise. But always go slowly. If you push psychic communication, or anything else, you will seem harsh, and will eventually frighten your dog.

Make certain that whenever you speak out loud to your dog you also give him silent signals. These should take the form of readily visible body movements. And, of course, these should be accompanied by thoughts: clear, precise, and to the point.

If you think you've received a silent communication from your dog, respond to it. Take the chance. If his messages go unheeded, he may stop sending them!

Thousands upon thousands of men, women, and children have had psychic relationships with their pets. Both you and your pet have the same potential; both you and your pet have so very much in common. Compared to the awesome variety of matter existent in the universe, humans and animals are really incredibly similar. If you try to have a psychic relationship with your pet, the chances are that you'll succeed.

PART TWO

Psychic Cats

Telepathic Cats

Perhaps the most telephatic and mysterious of all animals, cats have been whorshipped, feared, included in complicated rites and linked with strange superstitions. In fact, those who were once accused of witchery often were being accused only of consorting too closely with cats. To us, the cat, with his constant and unconscious grace, remains an ideal. There is not a ballerina alive who wouldn't want to move as fluidly as the most common housecat. The dexterity of the cat is a basis for certain schools of Oriental combat; and surely the Fastest Gun in Old Cheyenne would seem slow if his draw were compared to the lightning speed of a cat's most casual swipe! The cat remains a symbol for such Medieval holidays as Halloween; cats find their intelligent, inscrutable faces on the covers of occult magazines; and their profiles are used to suggest terror in tales of the supernatural. Truly, no animal has inspired such outpourings of affection from humans as has the cat—but neither has any other household animal quite so many enemies.

I grew up in a family in which everyone liked dogs and the only cats we had lived in the barn. I never knew what they did there, except to catch mice and to sleep beneath the cows' noses on the coldest nights so they might be warmed by the soft, bovine breath. While I had a certain affection for cats, I also had the usual misconceptions about the feline species which people who have not studied cats often have. I thought them disloyal, aloof, basically uninterested in human affairs. I don't exactly know what this says about me, but I wasn't terribly anxious to have a pet who was not loyal to me.

It wasn't until I went to college that I had my first real encounter with a cat—an encounter which lasted nine years. The cat in question—my first and all-important guide to the world of feline intelligence—picked me out in the late spring. He must have been only four or five months old, and as appealing as any of those cats whose pictures appear—usually with a ball of yarn, or wearing a gardening hat—on certain kinds of calendars. All gray, except for one white spot and a bit of white on the tip of his tail, this young cat had a somewhat Siamese body, yet a roundish face and a much fuller tail. There was no question that I found him appealing, yet there was also no question that I had no intention of keeping him.

In fact, I thought his survival mechanisms must have been a little off because he hadn't chosen a very likely candidate in his search for a suitable human companion. Nevertheless, I did give him a name—Alexander, or Alex—just so I'd have something to call him while I attended to the real business at hand—which was, of course, finding the home to which he belonged.

As time went on, and I met with no success in finding his true owners, a curious but undeniable soft spot for my little gray visitor appeared in my heart. Yet I was still determined to make his stay temporary.

Finally, I found a family who wanted Alex and I carried him the two blocks to their house. We said goodbye and I went off to my classes. When I returned home, Alex was waiting for me on the window sill. He ran down to greet me, making his prrt-prrt, and rubbing his arched back against my legs. I must admit I was glad to see him.

Still, I returned him to the family who'd adopted him and this time I didn't even say goodbye. Alex wasn't fooled by my outward behavior. He knew I liked him—he knew it better, and even before, I did. That evening he was waiting for me. Again I took him back to the family—who was getting a little bored with the complicated courtship—and this continued for a solid week before I gave in and told Alex he could live with me permanently.

The first thing I learned from Alex was the tremendous affection and fidelity cats are capable of showing. Perhaps it was because he'd been a stray and wasn't happy with the idea of separation; but, in no time, Alex had fitted himself very neatly into my schedule. He followed me to campus every day and, to my surprise, was waiting for me in roughly the same spot each afternoon, though my schedule of classes was changeable. Alex, however, knew when I'd be there. Only once was he late, and I could see him streaking toward our spot on the common—like an Olympic runner doing the 500 meters.

I was constantly amazed at how he seemed to know my daily schedule, though cat lovers know that felines have a knack for telling time. These cosmic creatures have intricate and unerring internal clocks. One black and white cat by the name of Gypsy is noted in the literature of the field. Gypsy's job was to wake his mistress at six forty-five every morning. However, when it was the season to switch to Daylight Saving Time, his mistress informed him, and Gypsy made the necessary adjustment.

The Gaddises, who have done a great service to the investigation into the secret world of animals through their writings, report a cat whose sense of human time helped the United States effort during World War II. This cat belonged to the governor of Idaho, whose wartime duty it was to make certain that local high school students showed up daily in the potato fields. When the governor's alarm clock broke, he found he didn't need a new one. His cat immediately assumed the unfailing responsibility of waking the governor every morning at seven o'clock sharp.

Dr. Gustav Eckstein of the University of Cincinnati relates the story of Willy, a feline strangely fascinated by the game of Bingo. Every Monday evening Willy would leave home at precisely seven thirty, trot across town to the hospital where the Bingo games were held, and stay until nine forty-five, at which time he thought he should be heading home. Willy's fascination with the game of Bingo is interesting in itself, but his sense of a weekly schedule is truly amazing.

(The cat's ability to achieve absolute oneness with the universe will be detailed fully in our discussion "The Cosmic Compass.")

But now, because my schedule was keeping me away from home more and more, I decided to find Alex a feline friend. I got Alex a little kitten to avoid contests that seem inevitable between grown cats. Alex thought this was a perfectly wonderful idea and he took to "Monk" immediately. Monk, an energetic tabby, looked up to Alex and it was a great pleasure to see them wrestling together, and staring at the things which only cats seem to see. For a while, I feared I might be excluded, but this was not the case. Alex was still fast friends with me.

One Saturday morning, I had to go to the drugstore and Alex, of course, came along. When I went inside, Alex, as usual, waited outside the door. A few minutes later, I noticed Alex was *in* the store, running down the aisle toward me in a state of tremendous agitation. Meowing loudly, his tail flicking like a whip, he stood before me. I didn't know if I was imagining it, but his eyes seemed bright with fear. I quickly put my purchases back on the shelf, picked up Alex, and took him outside. When I put him down, he began pacing back and forth, meowing louder and louder. Then he began to run—in the opposite direction from our house. He stopped in his tracks, meowed at me, and waited.

I knew Alex usually had a reason for doing the things he did and so I followed him. Alex took me farther and farther from our house until we came to a yard. He darted into the yard and crawled under an old, white frame house. I followed him, got on my knees, and tried to see what he was so concerned about.

When my eyes adjusted to the darkness, I saw Alex standing there over the motionless Monk. I reached under the building and lay my hand on Monk's chest. He was still breathing, but only slightly. There was blood on him; he'd been struck by a car.

I wish this story had a happy ending—but there was no saving the poor kitten. Yet my already immense respect for Alex grew even greater. How had he known the moment when disaster befell his friend Monk? What psychic distress signals had he received? And, if I had been more open, would I have "heard" Monk, too?

An English magazine called *Tomorrow* reports the same kind of phenomenon, but having to do with a cat's sensing a human's psychic distress call. A cat named Bill, devoted to his master, stayed home while his owner went traveling some distance. The man, badly hurt in a railway accident died in a hospital a few days later. He was buried near the hospital, and at the interment the man's brother saw Bill there.

Bill, the faithful and clairvoyant cat, had known what had happened, and had made the journey to be near his master. The cat went to the edge of the grave, looked at the coffin, and then, sadly, turned and went back home.

Since humans first stood face to face and looked long into the eyes of the feline, with its vertical pupil and endless multicolored depth, the cat has reminded us of the supernatural. The cat has always been associated with those parts of the universe which we humans fail to understand. When humans were closer to and still more or less remembered their animal (psychic) origins, it was not at all uncommon for animals to be worshipped as gods.

Dogs, crocodiles, species of birds, were all taken to represent the universal order and the hidden, secret powers of the universe. But no animal has been worshipped quite so fervently as the cat. In ancient Egypt, anyone known to have killed a cat was himself put to death.

For some, the quiet, secret grace of the cat may have been emblematic of all that was unknown in the universe; others may have been able to actually plumb the depths of the feline character, discovering all kinds of marvelous and astounding powers. It is interesting to note that as we drifted further and further from our origins, further from the animal kingdom, and developed our rational, logical explanations of the universe, worship of animals turned into *fear* of animals.

Medieval communities literally lived in dread of the wilderness that surrounded them. (See Chapter 11 on animal transformations for a more detailed look at this fear.) Animal nature, rather than being looked up to and learned from, became synonymous with godlessness and depravity. The cat, once placed upon a pedestal and revered for its psychic powers and infinite grace, was transformed into an evil omen; frightening creature of the night, companion of the devil and the devil's handmaidens, witches. The night patrolled by the cat was the night of the human unconscious; the psychological space the cat stalked was that of the innate psychic powers which humans had abandoned within themselves as they rushed headlong into the modern age.

But while we may have suffered from the evolutionary drift away from our psychic powers, the most common housecat impresses us as being not very different from his ancient ancestors. Ages of living with humans seem to have changed the cat very little. Perhaps the cat intuitively knew the dangers of domesticity and has, therefore, always kept part of himself in reserve. Even the pudgiest, most pampered show-cat lets us know in a hundred different ways that he is still an untamed creature, that he still primarily obeys a higher authority.

This does not mean that the cat is not a suitable or a loving pet. If you are going to have a truly close relationship with your cat, you must adopt your cat's ways of communication—and these are almost wholly psychic. Unlike a dog, you don't get close to a cat by rolling around on the floor with it, or throwing it sticks to chase (though many cats certainly enjoy both of these activities.) You will not even grow close to your cat by doing the things for it that it so manifestly demands—such as stroking it, feeding it, supplying it with catnip, and giving it the most luxurious spots to lounge and doze in. Your cat will definitely be pleased with all of these considerations; but if this is all your relationship consists of, it will be a limited one. The true closeness must come from a different direction: it must come from the psychic realm. True companionship with a cat is based on telepathic communication.

It is often said that cats are the most psychic of all the animals, more closely attuned to human thought and the natural order than even dogs. I see no reason to enter into this old dog-vs.-cat argument. All animals are psychic, and each species has a more profound psychic level than any human could hope to understand. However, to some people the private ways of the cat may be misread as a kind of inattention. Compared with dogs, most cats do seem a little antisocial, but it is this very aloofness which connects the cat so profoundly to the world of the unseen.

The cat is descended from solitary hunters (rather than from pack animals). This nature has caused it to depend to an extraordinary degree on its psychic abilities. Cats are designed for total awareness: it is their nature to respond to the slightest stimuli with utmost confidence and a complete lack of hesitation. This is true of cats in the wild, and it is true of domesticated cats as we've been told. A very highly regarded feline behaviorist and veterinarian once said to me, "The cat is a very psychic animal—it has to be, for survival. Its existence depends on acute psychic awareness."

Cats often appear nonchalant and abstracted because they don't depend on mere physical senses. Cats don't need to confirm the telepathic messages they receive. The cat is, as we have said, a total receiving organism—it is constantly receiving information at all points of its body and mind. That is why the cat sometimes seems the most schizophrenic of all creatures: it is at once sensual and hedonistic, aloof and cerebral. One moment, your cat can roll with pleasure at your gentle touch; the next he can be poised near the window, his ears flicking to messages only he can hear.

The cat divides his life between two worlds, and most strike a balance brilliantly. Our cats always seem to be dozing at the exact spot on the rug where the sun is the warmest—yet these same sensual creatures spend a portion of each day tuned in to messages which not only we can't hear but which remain a mystery to most other animals as well.

Cats are masters of foreknowledge, and our ability to heed the felines' predictions can either be amusing or life-saving. My cat Loretta, great-granddaughter of Alex, was uncanny in her ability to know whether the phone was ringing to herald a personal call or a business call. Loretta, a bit of an anarchist, would *never* respond to a business call, but if the call was personal Loretta would rush toward the ringing phone, and pace back and forth before it until I answered. When the person calling happened to be someone Loretta was fond of, she'd jump on the telephone table and touch the ringing instrument with the tip of her nose.

On a more crucial level, cats have been recorded as having sensed the presence of death and of predicting all manner of disasters. The British, who in World War II endured the Luftwaffe's bombs, learned to depend on their cats. It was widely observed that cats had a foreknowledge of bombing raids. Even before the approaching German planes were detected on radar, cats would be seen rushing toward bomb shelters. Although there is no official count of how many British lives were saved by heeding the warning of cats, it is widely agreed that the number is a high one.

In the area of animal heroism there seem to be many more recorded cases of dogs reaching out to save human or animal life than stories about cats. Quite simply, the cat's relatively small size makes its heroism less conspicuous. And the cat's reputation for unconcern with human affairs can lead people to ignore their warnings. If a dog senses danger it can, if need be, intervene directly. It can drag a child from a burning house, tug his master forcefully by the sleeve.

But the cat can only give signs and make small noises. Also, the cat's nature is not as similar to our own as is the dog's. While the cat can of course be loved and even worshipped, it is harder to identify with than the dog is. Few cat lovers can look at a pet and think: He's just like me! Even physically, where a dog may take on a striking resemblance to his owner, the cat will remain ever himself, will make only the most necessary modulations in his behavior so that he may communicate with his master. Cats have no intention of surrendering their individuality. They are supremely (and inspiringly) confident of themselves, of their completeness, of their profound understanding of the universal order.

However, when a cat needs to communicate it seems to make no difference who the listener is—the cat will try and will often succeed in getting the message across. W. A. Hudson tells the story of a cat who was raised with a puppy who became her closest friend. This cat was unusually small. When she had a litter of kittens, she found it difficult to carry them in her mouth. One day, for reasons known only to her, she suddenly judged her nest unsuitable, and a move to a new place became top priority in her life.

Since the birth of the kittens, her canine friend had been included in the family life. He often stood guard over the litter. While his instincts told him not to touch the kittens, it seemed from his gaze and attentions that he cared for them. But when it came time for the mother to move her nest she found that she needed her friend's assistance. She brought the dog face to face with her kittens, then walked with him to where she was making her new nest, then walked with him back to her litter. Although the dog seemed baffled, the mother cat left to continue preparing the nest. The dog did show up in the new nest, but without kittens. The mother cat led him to the old nest a second time. This time, the dog got her silent message. Going against all his instincts, he gently picked up and carried each kitten, moving the litter to its new home.

This is an instructive example of inter-species communication. Of course, to an expert, the cat explained her request to the dog through body language, but without a simultaneous telepathic communication the message would not have been complete nor would it have been understood. Clearly, the cat was able to transplant a visual image into the consciousness of her canine friend, a detailed and consecutive series of images which would at once encourage the dog to do a difficult thing and give him exact instructions of how to do it.

It seems to me that if a dog can learn to understand the unspoken language of a cat, we humans have a good chance of understanding it, too. A good start to learning to penetrate the sensitive and profound inner world of the cat is to concentrate on some of the outward signs and modes of communication that we can observe in any cat. The following chapter may help you begin.

Cat Language

A s we have said, our domestic cats carry the mark of aloneness inherited from their great cat ancestors. Cats sometimes hunt in groups, but there is no pack mentality. Though they have a strong sense of kinship, and are loving parents, cats like to hunt alone and a lot of their time resting and sleeping is also solitary. Cats are not anti-social—but because their senses are finely attuned to their inner lives and toward the perception of psychic phenomena, there is a limit to how much time they can spend being distracted by others.

Our pet cats reflect this independent nature and indeed many of them seem to have the souls of tigers. However, anyone who has gotten to know a cat understands that these imperious creatures are far from asocial. They merely demand respect, and this they have in common with practically all animals. The only difference is that cats know how to get it. Yet when your cat desires human contact, he's not at any loss for silent language. He knows how to let you know.

Cat body language is often quite subtle, but it can also be emphatic. When your cat decides it is time to make contact with you, he will march into the room and perform a veritable ballet to put this point across. There will be cheek-rubbing, and scraping of the entire body along the leg of a chair or the corner of a wall, the tail will be high and flicking, and in the throat will be rattling a high-pitched purr.

If you seem a little slow in catching on, your cat, hardly a prisoner of pride when it comes to his own needs, will leap onto your lap and continue the display at closer range. A happy cat will usually greet his owner at a lively trot, tail straight up, ears forward, and making meowing calls. This will probably be following by a forceful rubbing against your legs. This is the same contented dance most cats perform when they see that you are "finally" going to feed them—when it comes to mealtimes, cats like to accuse us of being a little bit late, even if they're not hungry! Two friendly cats who know each other well will use this same ritual to greet one another, and it's very similar to how the kitten greets and then tags along with his mother.

When I take my daily walk through the fields with my dogs and cats, I observe that the cats walk along in a supremely confident gait, their tails shooting up so high and straight that it seems that they'll lift their back paws off the ground. These walks, of course, have an element of chaos in them. The cats do a lot of aimless scampering, freezing and bolting in their perpetual duel with all of the things only they seem to see.

The dogs are scrambling and rough-housing, too, but in a more understandable fashion. However, if one of the cats lags too far behind, for any reason, the dogs' play will suddenly end. This is especially true for the female German Shepherd. She will wait with cocked ears until the cat **emerges** from the underbrush. If this doesn't happen soon, the dog will run over to investigate. Each time, the cat in question has been attending to the usual, invisible business of the average feline, but the dog's protective instincts haven't been dampened. She'll search the cat out, gaze into his eyes, touch noses, and then come running back, reassured.

This sense of responsibility and inter-species kinship is no one-way affair, by any means. The cat also feels very protective of the dogs. For example, a rather beautiful but definitely tough mongrel pays frequent social calls on my female dog—even though she is altered. Because this visitor is a better fighter than my male dog Eli, he will sadly take a background role, as the visitor and the female go through elaborate greetings and dances. Eli is capable of becoming depressed over these incidents, but he doesn't dare say anything—the sense of ranking connects with the sense of justice in the canine world.

But Eli need not worry because my cat Toastie has taken up his cause. Whenever the dashing mongrel comes to visit, Toastie will immediately put himself forward and, full of the puff and bluff of a warring cat, will hop sideways at the visiting dog, scaring him away through the sheer audacity of the tactic. Toastie treats no other dog this way, so I can only assume he is doing it for Eli. Toastie, in fact, is a miserable fighter and rather a pacifist—his little heart must pound with relief when the mongrel actually turns tail and leaves.

It is a common misconception that cats don't show much emotion on their faces, that their facial expression is severely limited and unreliable. Just as we spoke of the necessity of closely observing your canine companion, you cannot hope to form a deep understanding of your cat without a great deal of concentration on your part. Of course, the ultimate goal—the ultimate communication—is to meet your cat in the psychic realm. But before that kind of cosmic communication can be established, you'd better know as much about your cat's nature and outward signs as your cat knows about yours!

The cat is a very expressive creature, with a range and complexity to his emotions. The cat uses its total body to convey its state of mind—its pleasure, sexuality, rage, hunger, fear, doubt, suspiciousness, playfulness and affection. When a cat's in good spirits it is virtually irresistible. Nature seems to have provided no other creature with such an effective repertory of flirtations. We've already described some of the ways a domestic cat will solicit the attentions of his master. It's interesting, I think, to observe how much more cautious cats are among themselves. It's as if they know we need louder, more direct instructions.

Two familiarized cats, even with a history of kinship, will be generally tentative in their initial greetings. Stepping carefully forward, they will extend their noses and then briefly touch. There is a quick sniffing of lips and at the side of the head. Both of these places have glands called the perioral glands which radiate identifying scents. (These same glands are stimulated when your cat rubs his face against the leg of a chair or against *your* legs.) If all indications are positive, the greeting will continue. The ears will remain forward, the tails will be relaxed. They will continue to rub their cheeks together, drinking in and approving of each other's olfactory signatures. The inspection and identification may go even further, progressing to the tail where the caudal gland, is located and to the anus, location of the perianal gland.

Cats display aggression or fear in varied ways. The ambivalent cat will now take up the defensive stance, which will be a semi-crouch, with the body turned at a slightly sideways angle. The ears will stand outward and horizontal (much like a matador's cap!) and the growls will be deep and menacing. This is the time when your cat longs to be larger, and it almost seems as if he were remembering the time when he was a 500-pound beast. To compensate for his size, he will puff up and make his hairs stand on end. His pupils will dilate and if this terrible display isn't enough to ward off the feared or hated object, the growl will rise in pitch, until it is a blood-curdling yowl. The ears will lie even flatter and the eyes will widen still more. If the object of all this is another cat, the aggressor cat will be going through pretty much the same ritual.

A fight under these circumstances is not always inescapable. But even without actual physical conflict, crucial information is being exchanged about the character, status, and flexibility of the respective felines.

Facial expressions in your cat vary widely and indicate quite specific states of being. The direct stare, for instance, is not a gesture of forwardness or species friendliness. Generally, when your cat gazes unblinkingly into your eyes, he is trying to put you back in your own psychological space, to distance himself from you. If the stare is particularly intent it is a semi-aggressive sign, a way of letting you know that contact would not only be considered an imposition but an affront! Glancing eyes, or averted eyes, interspersed with lowered ears in an expression of submission, often given when your cat is caught in the act of doing something he knows he oughtn't.

(By the way, a common myth about cats is that they are oblivious to our concepts of right and wrong. This is really not so. They might not always accept the wisdom behind our judgments of right and wrong but it is a rare cat who doesn't know the difference. The Gaddises tell the story of Timothy, a cat who ate his mistress's pet canary. He was punished, of course, and kicked out of the house. When Timothy returned "he carried, unharmed, a nestling sparrow which he deposited at the feet of his mistress.")

Another central cat expression, and one that strikes many as looking somewhat comical, comes with arousal from the scent of something that seems very important to the cat—such as the scent of another cat, or a plate of expensive cheese. Your cat will take deep sniffs, his eyes will become heavily-lidded, and his jaw will open, allowing his tongue to droop slightly out. Tom will then turn from the scent a little, open his eyes, and seem to stare blankly into space. He is using an important organ located behind his two incisor teeth, called the vomeronasal organ, or Jacobson's organ. By opening his mouth, your cat is recording and inspecting the scent with yet another faculty.

During times of contentment, or social cleaning with another cat, or when being lovingly patted by you, Tom will half-close his eyes and an inner eye membrane will appear, clouding the eye and giving him an expression of supreme relaxation. This glazed, "stoned" expression generally accompanies Tom's major pleasure, playing with you, copulating, eating imported ham, etc. The most delightful expression, though, is that of a cat ready to play: the eyes are wide, pupils dilated, and a glance that seems almost ironic. The ears are straight forward, and the head pokes out from the body. The nose, too, becomes active, pushing forward while the nostrils occasionally expand and contract.

In a close relationship with a human friend, the object is to communicate with you, the cat will expand or modify his body language, invent behaviors and abolish others. Of course, the cat has to have the sense that his signals are being attended to, studied and remembered, but once this is established you will see modifications in body language as the cat learns shortcuts to your understanding and apprehends, as well, what you will and will not respond to.

When I approach my cat Toastie and put my face near his and begin scratching his back if he does not wish to mingle with me at that moment, he will make it clear by closing his eyes and giving me a light tap on the cheek with his paw. By closing his eyes, he is telling me there is nothing serious or aggressive about his tap, nor is any particular disrespect intended. When one of the dogs approaches him at a time when he is not feeling like being entertained, he will inform them of his mood in much the same way.

The voice is an important mode of communication in the world of the feline. Though students of the subject cannot decide why exactly it is that a cat purrs, the purr is generally accepted as a sign of contentment. It is most often linked to times of social cleaning or petting, but it can also be elicited by a clink of a spoon against a feeding dish, or the entrance of a favorite person.

Cat language is an intriguing mixture of surface simplicity and submerged complexities. Roughly speaking, there are three major types of feline vocalizations: the purr, the meow, and the yowl. But within these three major modes of sounds, there are, to be certain, hundreds of variations, hundreds of subtleties.

For example, the yowl of a cat who is beginning a stand-off with another cat he feels he can subdue is quite a different sound from the yowl of a cat beginning a losing battle. The meow of a cat before a closed door is quite a different sound from the meow of a cat who has just caught a mouse, though both of these sounds would have to be categorized as meows—or, as some students of the subject call them, *vowel sounds*.

In order for all of these differences to make real sense to you, and in order to enter into the world of the cat, you must open your ears—including your inner ears—to the slightest gradations of emphasis and intonation, and observe closely the circumstances surrounding the vocalization of your cat. If you think it's all just a lot of random chatter then you'll never understand your cat's language. But if you grant that there is reason and coherence in the vocalizations then you will come to understand them.

Just as you can (and should) observe and learn Tom's language, your cat is learning in depth your body language and the hidden messages of *your* vocalizations. He is ever observant when it comes to your behavior and he learns quickly. For instance, he can distinguish without much difficulty, the way your footsteps sound when you are angry, how they sound when you are just strolling to the refrigerator. Tom can tell by the way you stretch in bed if you are soon going to get up, or good for another hour's lazing and dozing. Your every indication, through your body language, as well as the force of your unconscious thoughts being telepathically transmitted, informs him of the nature of your mood or what your intentions are. The way you sit in your chair tells Tom about you. The rate of your breathing, your sighs, all of these things relay specific information to your observant cat.

When a cat owner is communicative with the cat, it facilitates the cat's understanding and makes for a more socially involved and comfortable animal. When verbal communication becomes a part of the relationship, the cat becomes that much more attentive and responsive. Your cat's nature is to understand his environment, and you are central to it. When spoken to, your cat will come to feel more included, more engaged in the daily life of you and the household. Will he come to talk back to you? Probably yes, though he may match your verbal communication with body language, or even increased attempts to communicate telepathically.

In studying cat language, Gillette Grilhe, a well-known authority on the subject, has written that cats make sixty-three distinct sounds. But it appears that their understanding vocabulary is much larger. Jhan Roberts, in his *Your Pet's Secret Language*, quotes psychologist Dr. Milton Kreutzer as saying that cats can understand more than a hundred words in English. Among them are *dinner, beautiful, dog, garbage, head, kiss, play, toy, water,* and *yes.* Some of

---

the more exotic words in the cat vocabulary are *pillow, typewriter, vacuum cleaner, counter, sweep* and *undress.*

This kind of communication is indispensable to a close and active relationship with your cat. It involves a lot of commitment and a lot of effort—and perhaps it is because it calls for those two things that it *is* so important. The work done to establish rapport on the level of the five everyday senses is the perfect and crucial preliminary for communication on the plane of the sixth sense—the most remarkable and eternal communication. The next chapter will give a better indication of what lies in store for those who make psychic contact with their pets!

PART THREE

Cosmic Cohorts

The Cosmic Compass

A s we study animals and learn from them about ourselves, we become increasingly aware of how much we are capable of and how much we have forgotten. Of all the talents or instincts from which we have evolved, one of the most remarkable is the ability to know exactly where we stand in relation to our surroundings.

Human beings are makers of maps, markers, flags, compasses, signposts—all designed to mark and record our relationships to the vastness of physical space. For all of the pains we go through to chart the pathways of our lives, we still are apt to get lost. Families on camping trips perish in the woods; a man driving on a familiar highway can accidentally take a wrong turn and have no idea where he is.

When we stop to consider the enormous efforts we have made throughout the centuries to, quite simply, figure out where we are, it is all the more amazing that the animal kingdom is filled with creatures who travel enormous distances with no other guidance but their own internal sense of navigation and a fixed, instinctual understanding of how the space which they occupy relates to the vastness of all space.

Scientists have long been fascinated by the ability of animals to navigate long distances without error. Despite years of study, no special part of the animal nervous system appears to have been designed for this task. And so, it is more than likely that animals' phenomenal acts of navigation are psychic in origin. It is for this reason that many of the pioneers in this field referred to this ability as psi-trailing, meaning, trailing through psychic (psi) power.

One scientist who has taken a long and amazed look at animal navigation is Dr. Michael Fox, America's best-known animal psychologist. Fox offers for our consideration in his excellent book *Understanding Your Dog* the case of certain eels who are reared in fresh water, but then migrate to the Sargasso Sea when it is time to mate. From there, the eel offspring make their way back inland to the fresh waters from which their parents came—but they make this journey totally on their own, with no adults to guide them.

The flights of the monarch butterfly are every bit as amazing. This lovely but tiny-brained creature migrates South before laying its eggs, and then dies. When the monarch's offspring are born, they migrate back to North America, where their parents came to maturity. But what's even more astonishing is that on the long journey North the monarch butterflies pause in particular trees, used traditionally in the migration of their species. Each year, these same trees fill up with new generations of butterflies. The native Americans thought these trees had special, spiritual qualities.

Each small section of the planet has its own special relationship to the sun—a relationship that is, of course, in constant transition as the earth goes through its orbit.

Dr. Fox writes: "If an animal can perceive the time and regulate its activities in accordance with the time of day or the season, it should be able to find the square mile where it lives by 'reading' the sun and the angle of its rays in relation to the expected value that its internal clock anticipates. Incongruity is met with motivation to reduce the dissonance between solar and internal time. And the translocated animal is able to find his square mile on the globe."

Clearly, many feats of migration are a function of the animal's awesome fine tuning with the sun. Bees, for instance, can follow the sun even on overcast days because they are sensitive to the rays of polarized light. This pairing off of an uncanny—and as yet unknown—internal clock with the journey of the sun also seems to play a major role in such remarkable migrations as those experienced by seals, caribou, elephants and turtles.

Yet other animals display a finely tuned cosmic clock and they do it without any benefit of the sun's rays. Rachel Carson, renowned naturalist and ecologist, studied a flatworm called the convoluta, which is a life partner with the sea's green algae. Whenever the tide goes out, the convoluta is sure to emerge from the sand and expose its green body to the sun. Carson brought samples of these creatures to her laboratory and was fascinated to learn that the little flatworms continued their inflexible schedule. "Without a brain, or what we would call a memory," comments Carson, "or even a very clear perception, convoluta continues to live out its life in this alien place, remembering, in every fibre of its small green body, the tidal rhythm of the distant sea."

My first experience with psi-trailing came several years ago. My sister in Burlington, Vermont, was forced, for a number of reasons, to give up her collie-retriever mix. Through contacts with good friends, my sister was able to find Bonnie a good home in a small farming community about seventy miles away. (Neither my sister nor Bonnie had even been to this town before.)

Several days before Bonnie was to be delivered to her new home, she became very aggressive and ill-mannered—snapping at guests, chewing slippers, moaning and whimpering without apparent cause. This worried my sister, to be sure, but she went ahead with the plan to bring Bonnie to the dog's new home. The dog's new owner was thrilled with her new pet and admired Bonnie's beauty and readily perceived intelligence. Even Bonnie seemed to perk up at her new master's praise. My sister bid the dog adieu and left, sniffling back tears of parting. Bonnie watched her, whining beneath her breath.

Three days later, Bonnie greeted my sister at their old homestead, looking healthy, spry, and very proud. My sister was stunned. The love and devotion that had motivated and guided Bonnie over that

---

long distance—over land and lake, across unfamiliar territory—seemed suddenly more important than all thoughts of convenience or practicality. After some soul-searching, my sister changed her plans and made room for Bonnie so the dog might take its rightful place in her household.

How did Bonnie find her way? It is possible, for those who understand the fierce love of which pets are capable, to understand why she'd want to, or even need to make the trip—but through what secret intelligence did she find her way? While science has given us the glimmerings of an understanding when it comes to the yearly, inbred migrations of whole animal populations, the many extraordinary tales of psi-trailing remain unexplained. Unexplained, that is, by any other theory except that of psychic power.

One of the most thoroughly documented cases of psi-trailing is that of Sugar, a cream-colored cat of Persian ancestry. Sugar had a slight deformity in his left hipjoint which could be felt when he was petted, though the deformity never seemed to bother the cat. Sugar was owned by the Woods family, who lived in Anderson, California. Upon retirement, Mr. Woods arranged to move to Gage, Oklahoma, to live on a farm. The Woodses knew from experience that their cat was terrified of automobiles and it would be, they all agreed, quite a chore to get Sugar to take the 1500-mile ride.

Sure enough, while the packing was being finished the Woodses saw Sugar leap from the car and run. It was manifestly impossible to force Sugar to endure the drive, and so the Woods family left Sugar with some neighbors with whom he was familiar and who liked the cat a great deal.

The following year, about fourteen months after the separation in California, Sugar appeared at the farm in Oklahoma—nearly 1500 miles, to a place he'd never been before. Of course, the Woods family at first didn't believe it was their cat. They had missed Sugar so they could only be delighted by the similarity. They played with the newcomer and the cat seemed completely at home and relaxed with them. Of course, there must have been speculations about the cat, moments when his resemblance to Sugar seemed too remarkable to be meaningless, but it was not until Mrs. Woods was idly stroking the cat and found the tell-tale protruding hipbone that they realized that the cat was undeniably Sugar.

The Woodses got in touch with the California family with whom they'd left Sugar, and were told that Sugar had indeed disappeared three weeks after the Woods family had left for Oklahoma. Sugar had taken a thirteen-month and one-week pilgrimage to his heart's mecca—the family he loved.

Dr. J.B. Rhine of Duke University became interested in Sugar's remarkable journey, and came to Oklahoma to observe Sugar and gather data. Dr. Rhine was so amazed and impressed that he requested that upon Sugar's death the body be sent to Duke University. Alas, this never came to pass. Sugar left home one day on a routine hunting expedition and never returned. The chances are that he met with something in the forest which overpowered him, though it is tempting to postulate that his psychic knowledge of an eternity spent in a university biological lab might have prompted his disappearance. The unknown has an odd way of protecting itself.

The psi-trailing abilities of pets have always astounded and fascinated humans. But is it so incredible? Only if we insist that animal navigation has a 100% biological basis do the feats of animals remain a puzzle. The African cuckoo, for instance, a migrating bird, is left by its mother in a nest of a bird of another species, hatched and raised by its foster mother, and then, with no assistance, searches out and joins the migrational patterns of his parents. Likewise, the homing ability of pigeons has long baffled scientists, and has been studied and tested for at least a century. Attempts to "fool" the birds have been made. They've been placed in unfamiliar territory, and sure enough, nearly all find their way home without much difficulty—without ruffling a feather, as it were!

Unfortunately, the vast majority of studies made of animal navigation have proceeded with what I call a "quantitative bias." That is to say, the testers have looked for something that could be measured, isolated, represented on a graph. To the detriment of all, most science is not geared to the explanation of those questions whose answers cannot be neatly stated or measured.

Later on, we will have an up-to-date report on how ESP experiments are being conducted in the world's laboratories. But for now it remains to be mentioned at science's insistence that only magnetism or light sensitivity can be responsible for the astounding acts of navigation so many animals are capable of, has meant that for the most part the official explanations of this phenomenon have been woefully incomplete.

One scientist who has remained open to the psychic realm is Duke University's Dr. J.B. Rhine. Investigating the homing abilities of pigeons, Dr. Rhine reports the case of a pigeon owned by a young boy named Hugh Perkins. One day a banded pigeon flew into Hugh's backyard. The bird, though bearing an identifying mark, did not seem eager to leave. After a while, Hugh began to feed the bird, as well as speaking gently to it. To Hugh's delight the bird responded to him and their relationship developed and deepened over the year. But suddenly, Hugh fell ill and his parents rushed him over the mountains to a hospital a full hundred and twenty miles away.

The next night, while recuperating from his emergency operation, Hugh heard a gentle tapping on the window of his room. When he turned, he saw a pigeon standing on the windowsill, its feet stiff in the West Virginia snow. The bird stayed there all through the night. The next morning a nurse came into the room and Hugh was able to ask her to open the window. In flew his beloved pigeon, with the identifying band on its iridescent leg.

How, Dr. Rhine wonders, did the bird know where Hugh was? How did he find his way over the mountains? How did he find the exact sill to light upon, a hundred and twenty miles away?

In the animal kingdom psi-trailing is an essential survival skill, linked either to the nomadic style of life of certain animals or held in reserve for circumstance. Using the psychic sense, animals are able to find a lost or injured mate over hundreds of miles. Tracking down a lost cub; finding water; vacating grazing grounds before natural disaster strikes—all of these common acts of animals in the wild call for the use of the sixth sense.

For our pets, it is no different. When lost or translocated, they will in effect tune down their other senses so that their sixth sense might come to the forefront, because clearly this sense is the only sure and accurate way to find their way home.

Sometimes this occurs in a backwards manner, as in the case of Mastic the cat. Mastic's owners moved to a new home one hundred and sixty miles away. Mastic was either bewildered by the move, or he just plain didn't approve of it. Whatever Mastic's motive, he soon left his new home and made his way over the miles of unfamiliar terrain, back to his former dwelling place. As I said, we can only guess at Mastic's motive. I've known too many cats to ever feel comfortable in stating exactly why they do the things they do. Mastic, however, was unstoppably determined to return to his old home.

Cats often find it terribly difficult to move with their owners to a new home. Most of this reversal type psi-trailing is done by cats, and it is for this reason that some people believe that cats are actually more attached to specific points on the earth than they are to their human companions.

But for the most part our pets have great faith in us, and will do just about anything to remain with us. One particularly moving report involves a family living in an apartment in heavily populated Manhattan. They'd taken a summer house some hundred miles away, and like most loyal owners, they'd taken their cat with them. The cat took to the country life—so much so that she became pregnant before the summer was over.

Unfortunately, the time for the family's return coincided with the time for the cat to give birth to her litter. Like many cats, she had already found and prepared a secret nest in which to give birth. On departure day, she was nowhere to be found and so, with heavy heart, the family made their way back to the city without her.

A little under two months later, the cat appeared at the window of their second story apartment. She carried one of her kittens in her mouth. Mother and kitten had traveled the hundred miles—through fields, towns, and, finally, through the chaotic heart of Manhattan. The family was overjoyed and astonished but their celebration was cut short. Before long, the mother cat was gone again. She turned up two weeks later, with another of her kittens in her teeth. This time, the family put her in the car, and they drove back to the country house to collect the rest of the litter!

The so-called internal clock, which many say all creatures are endowed with, seems to be a reasonable theory explaining the migration of certain species, but it does not cover the essentials of psi-trailing—especially psi-trailing that involves a pet seeking out a place to which he or she has never been. The internal clock may be an excellent device for perceiving a way back home; but, as we've seen, this simple explanation does not begin to clear up the mystery of hundreds of uncanny migration incidents.

One such incident involved a dog named Bobbie, who had to find his way home against what would seem like insurmountable odds.

Bobbie and his owner were on vacation, driving East from their home in Oregon. When they reached the town of Wolcott, Indiana, Bobbie suddenly spied a dog-fight in progress. With a great instinctual leap, he was out the car window. By the time his owners had gathered their wits, the local dogs, undoubtedly annoyed by Bobbie's intrusion, had chased Bobbie away. Bobbie's owners searched for him, but to no avail. They gave up—in a way that most dogs would not give up on their masters—and continued on their way. When it was time to return to Oregon they took a wholly different route, through Mexico.

Six months later, Bobbie reached home, skinny and utterly exhausted. There was no mistaking the dog's identity. In fact, affidavits by the Humane Society and other accounts proved the amazing fact that Bobbie did not retrace the route taken to Indiana, nor did he follow the route through Mexico. Instead, Bobbie had turned around and headed straight for Oregon, covering and conquering such awesomely rugged territory as the Rocky Mountains!

Of course, there are countless cases that have gone eternally unresolved. Often newspapers will report the heart-rending case of a dog fixed in one spot because he'd been told to stay by a master who then disappeared, or who was unable to use his psychic channels to get back to his master or home territory.

Such was the case of the unnamed sheepherding dog who sat along a highway in Ohio, always facing with deep, longing eyes the long hilly road. It was obvious to all who passed the dog that he waited for an absent master. By night, the dog would leave his fixed spot, probably to hunt for food. But by daybreak, the loyal, patient dog would be back at his post along the highway, again facing in the same direction. He was cordial to the local people, many of whom petted him and brought him food, but no matter how they tried to lure him away with offers of shelter and love, he would only politely refuse and maintain his vigil.

Another nameless hound took up a similar roadside residence, only this time the scene was set in England. The dog had lived between two directional signs for years, seemingly wanting no company and awaiting his master's return. Finally, people of the area donated a dog-house to help him through the rains and the winter winds. They also began feeding the dog, who seemed grateful. But nevertheless, he lacked all interest in re-establishing roots, or relating to the local people.

Stories such as these are fascinating, I think, because they are not truly explained by what is known of animal behavior. Dogs for the most part are not loners. Of their own accord, one would think that some of those waiting canines would have hooked up with a local dog-pack, or allowed themselves to be adopted by the people who were invariably moved by the sight of a lonely vigilant dog, staring at an empty road.

It seems that many pets are not fully capable of making use of their psychic powers. Animals, like humans, appear to have varying levels of psychic capacity. This variance in psi-trailing ability may account for the pets who get lost and never find their way home. Other contributing factors can be a lack of confidence in general—

extending even to the other five senses. But a major obstacle to using their sixth sense to psych their way home is the fact that a pet's master did not have open channels for psychic communication with the lost animal—even though he may have loved the pet very much. Love is the necessary base for any relationship, but love also needs open communication. Without this link between pet and human, the connection between the two is vulnerable and can collapse during a time of crisis, emergency, or separation.

Sometimes psi-trailing and deep psychic communication between pet and human can lead to such heartening stories as the tale of the dog named Shep. Shep was owned by Francis McMahon. One day, as Francis had started down the basement stairs to make some repairs, Shep suddenly began barking. Though this seemed a little out of character for Shep, Francis assumed it was unimportant and continued downstairs. Suddenly he lost his balance and tumbled down the flight. He was taken to the hospital, and Shep followed along. Shep was in the corridor when Francis was wheeled out of the Emergency Room, and he was able to tell Shep that everything was all right. He ordered Shep to wait for him, which Shep did. But Francis's condition grew worse, and within hours he died. His body was wheeled out the hospital rear entrance while poor Shep waited where he'd been told to. At the moment Francis's body was taken from the hospital, Shep began to bark —loudly, piteously, tragically, in a despairing farewell.

Shep waited in the hospital vicinity for twelve years. Only his own death could end his vigil. While it seemed clear that he knew something terrible had befallen his master, Shep chose to live with unyielding hope.

EIGHT

Animals Who Take the Step Beyond

It's a rare person who cannot learn from animals. If I leave no impression in this book other than that close concentration on the complex world of our pets can teach us about ourselves—our past, our potential, I will be more than satisfied. The true and exciting world of psychic pets exists here and now—with you and your own pet. But to give a better idea of the range of animal behavior, these next two chapters will relate some intriguing and well-documented cases which help to define the wide boundaries of animal behavior.

Our first story is not really connected with our exploration of the psychic realm, but I include it here because it emphasizes how animals can educate us in the most unexpected ways. The education in this case is a moral one, and the pupil is none other than Napoleon Bonaparte. Here, in Napoleon's own words, is what happened after a bloody battle:

"Suddenly I saw a dog emerging from under the greatcoat of a corpse. He rushed toward us, then returned to his retreat uttering mournful cries. He licked the face of his former master and darted toward us again; it seemed as if he was seeking aid and vengeance at the same time. Whether it was my state of mind, or the silence of the guns, the weather, the dog's act itself or I know not what, never has anything on a field of battle made such an impression on me. I stopped involuntarily to contemplate the spectacle; that man, I said to myself, perhaps had friends, perhaps he had them in our camp, in his Company; and yet, he lies here abandoned by all except his dog. What is man? And what the mystery of of his emotions? I had ordered battles without hesitation, battles which were to decide the fate of the Army; I had seen, dry-eyed, movements executed which resulted in the loss of a great number of our soldiers; but here and now, that dog moved me to tears."

The story of a German Shepherd named King, documented in 1975, shows us something of a dog's view of death. King was owned by a family who ran a small store; his strongest attachment was to the grandfather. As the old man drifted toward death, King looked on, growing daily more silent and mournful. When the grandfather died, King burst into a full-throated mourning—howling, whining, and barking. Yet, strangely, all of this was accompanied by his insistent scratchings on the door.

What made King's behavior especially puzzling was that his friend had been no longer in view—the family had been keeping the dying man downstairs behind the store. On the day of the funeral King got out of the house and bolted. The family searched for him and continued to search for three weeks—but to no avail. Finally, someone remembered how intensely emotional King had been at the grandfather's passing and it was proposed that they look for King at the cemetery. They went to where the grandfather was buried and asked the groundskeeper if he'd seen a German Shepherd. Yes, said the groundskeeper, and he described King and said he came every day. Each afternoon at two o'clock King approached his beloved friend's grave, where he would stand or lie, moaning, howling, or whining. However, if anyone tried to approach King during his ritual of grief, King would growl menacingly.

Among all the many stories of extraordinary pets, the story of a dog named Chris is one of the most remarkable. Chris was tested hundreds of times for his powers of ESP and in at least one series of tests his score was such that his testers said that if it was partially luck or accident, such a high percentage could not be duplicated more than once in a hundred billion times.

Chris was two years old when he was given to a Rhode Island man named George Woods. Chris, a beagle-mix, was active to the point of being frenetic. It was not at all uncommon for the honey-colored dog to be racing wildly all about the house. Mr. Woods was heard to say, "That dog acted crazy. If he had been a child, we'd have taken him to a psychiatrist."

The family who had owned Chris originally had been large and active, with a number of children. George Woods and his wife Marian decided that perhaps Chris had been neglected, or somehow lost in the shuffle of his former home. They decided that the dog might settle down if they gave him a secure feeling of affection. George Woods was the chief chemist and research director for a local textile plant, and was away at work all day. Marian, an artist, was generally home, where she gave a few painting lessons. Slowly, they absorbed the hyperactive Chris into their quiet domesticity.

When Chris was five years old a guest arrived with a dog who could "speak" its own name by tapping out the appropriate number of letters with its paw. This talented dog could also solve simple arithmetic problems. Chris watched with apparent fascination—he had never been taught even simple dog tricks. When the exhibition was over, Mrs. Woods turned to Chris and said, "Well, suppose you tell us Chris—how much is two and two?"

Chris looked for a moment and then touched Mrs. Woods' arm four times with his paw.

Within a short time Chris was able to rap out numbers with great speed. He was quite capable of doing sums—as long as they weren't too complex. But as his arithmetical abilities improved over the next couple of months, Mr. Woods brought home engineers and scientists from his workplace so they might watch (and be amazed by) his surprising dog.

Soon Chris learned the alphabet—tapping his paw once for 'A,' twice for 'B,' and so on. Chris correctly answered questions by which the Woodses themselves were stumped. In fact, it became less and less important to Chris *who* was interrogating him. There were about twenty people with whom he could easily relate and whose questions he would answer. Reporters frequently came to the Woodses home to "interview" Chris. The Woodses, naturally proud, kept these stories in a scrapbook. Chris also became something of a TV star, appearing on such programs as "The Gary Moore Show." He also performed on the cabaret circuit and in "concert." All of the money earned by Chris went to charities such as the ASPCA—the American Society for Prevention of Cruelty to Animals.

All was not completely high-minded in Chris's life. A neighbor of the Woods family, a woman known as Miss Goulding, asked Chris to tell her who would win the next day's Daily Double to be run at Narragansett. Miss Goulding had no particular interest in horse-racing or betting, but she did pay close attention when Chris tapped out the winners with his paw. She listened to him—placed the bets—and won!

This seemed to be talent of a different order, and Miss Goulding urged the Woodses to call in Dr. Henry F. Nugent of a nearby school of education. Dr. Nugent ran tests on Chris. Later, Dr. Renu J. Caboret and Dr. Pratt, both of Duke University, came to continue the testing.

The scientists from Duke tested Chris with ESP (or Zener) cards—a deck of twenty-five, using variations of five symbols: circle, cross, wavy lines, stars and squares. The Duke researchers, while undoubtedly impressed by Chris's ability to do sums and his mastery of the alphabet, were more interested in testing his powers of ESP. In this respect, Chris's test scores were astronomically high! Time after time, Chris selected the card bearing the symbol of which the doctors were thinking.

George and Marian Woods took pains that Chris's notoriety did not interfere too much with the simple canine pleasures he so enjoyed. He roamed freely through the neighborhood, choosing as his special friend, a German Shepherd and pointedly ignoring a French Poodle who Chris said was D-U-M-B. He had a terrible weakness for chasing cars and stubbornly persisted in this habit, despite the Woodses insistence that he stop. However, when he disappeared for a while and George or Marian asked if he'd been chasing cars, he owned up to his misbehavior and tapped out Y-E-S.

In 1959, the remarkable Chris was stricken with a heart attack. He continued to be tested for his ESP abilities and his awesome powers did not diminish even as his health slowly failed. Unfortunately, his last test for ESP revealed a slight falling off of his sixth sense: Chris was one day off on his prediction of the date of his own death.

We've seen a number of dogs who have mastered the art of learning a code through which they can communicate with people. But this leap across the species-barrier is not the exclusive skill of dogs—it most often happens with canines because of the special relationship humans have formed with dogs.

But in a book entitled *The Psychic Realm* is told the story of Lady Wonder, a filly whose desire to make her mind and its powers known to humans, inspired her to learn to use a typewriter. It was not, of course, a normal typewriter: the keys were fashioned of soft rubber and were very large. Lady Wonder touched the keys with her muzzle. Lady Wonder was, to be sure, a sensation and the local papers gave her exploits more space than it did to the return of Admiral Byrd!

In 1932, a reporter for the Richmond *News Leader* named Katherine Warren was sent to interview Lady Wonder. Here are some of the questions and answers:

KW: Can you tell me whether there will be any bad calamities in the U.S. during the coming year?

LW: Yes.

KW: What will they be?

LW: Storms.

KW: Will they do any damage in Virginia?

LW: Sure.

KW: Can you tell me who will be nominated by the Democrats for President?

LW: Roo—(Here she stopped typing and looked around) I can't spell the name.

During that same interview, Lady Wonder spelled out Katherine

Warren's middle name, though the name was unknown to her trainer. The wonder horse also typed out two numbers known only to Warren and her companion written on a concealed slip of paper.

In 1946, Dr. Thomas Garrett, a New York City psychologist, came to see Lady Wonder. Dr. Garrett was skeptical—in fact, he had come to see the astonishing filly in connection with a book he was writing which was to be an exposé of various supernatural phenomena. Whatever Dr. Garrett's opinion turned out to be about the so-called Supernatural Phenomena of the world, it did not take long for him to be overwhelmingly convinced of Lady Wonder's extraordinary power. Lady Wonder told Garrett that he had received a long distance phone call in which the operator had told Garrett that a man named Murphy was trying to contact him. Lady Wonder knew more than this. She typed out the information that Murphy's first name was Pat, and that he was married to an actress named Diane Ross. Garrett checked immediately with a New York theatrical agent and ascertained there was indeed an actress named Diane Ross. When he asked if Diane Ross was married, he was informed that she was—to a man named Pat Murphy!

Lady Wonder regularly and successfully predicted the results of horse races. When news of the equine tipster's activities spread, her efforts were called to a halt by racing officials. Lady Wonder's owners, still interested in capitalizing on the horse's psychic abilities, set up a kind of side-show in their barn, charging the curious a dollar for each question they put to the amazingly intelligent horse.

Like any human psychic, who can't be always 100% correct, Lady Wonder was not invariably accurate in her answers to questions put to her. But her successes were impressive, and in a number of cases, invaluable.

She foresaw the entry of the U.S. and Russia into World War II at a time when many political experts were predicting the opposite. She predicted the victory of Harry Truman in the famous 1948 election—an event analyzed incorrectly by nearly all commentators.

In 1951, her help was sought in locating a four-year-old named

Danny Matson who had mysteriously disappeared from his home in Quincy, Massachusetts. Lady Wonder said the child was in the area of "Pitts' Field." Investigators immediately searched the Pittsfield, Massachusetts area. Not finding little Danny, they thought that the horse had misled them. Then it was realized that nearby was a quarry known as Field and Wilde's Pit. Searchers were immediately dispatched—and the strayed little Danny Matson was found and rescued. Chances are he would have perished there if Lady Wonder hadn't somehow learned his whereabouts.

One of the most bewildering reports of animal intelligence I've ever read about was reported in *Fate*, a magazine devoted to the recording of true (and remarkable) tales of nature. The main character in this strange drama was a mongoose known as Gref, who lived on the Isle of Man. Amazingly, the Gref could *speak*. To get a sense of Gref's volatile personality, consider the story of the psychic investigator who traveled from the English mainland to look into accounts of Gref's abilities.

When the British researcher appeared at Gref's island home, the eerie mongoose promptly urinated on the man's foot and screamed, "Go away, clear to hell! We don't want you here!"

Gref's life among humans was never an easy one. One day, he wandered into a farmhouse owned by James T. Irving in a section of the Isle of Man called Doarl Cashen. Like a typical mongoose, Gref lodged in the Irvings' walls and began to make a nuisance of himself. The mongoose's scratchings and vocalizings were extremely irritating. Before long, Mr. Irving began to plot the intruder's demise. What Irving didn't know, of course, was that not only could Gref hear him, but could also *understand* Irving's plan. One day, while Irving was denouncing the pest in his walls, Gref repeated Irving's words verbatim in a voice pitched a couple of octaves higher than a woman's.

This understandably rattled the Irvings. It was decided to abandon the plan to kill the mongoose. Soon the truce developed into a kind of grudging affection by the Irvings for the creature. They began leaving food for Gref, and Gref reciprocated by leaving his fresh kills for the Irvings at their farmdoor. He also did them the favor of ridding their house of mice. He scared the rodents away by meowing like a cat!

The Irvings began to talk to Gref through the walls, but Gref refused to let them see him. In his own words, he said he couldn't consort with them because he was "a freak, a ghost and part of the fifth dimension." But when they pressed him on the subject Gref admitted that he was really reluctant to show himself because of Mr. Irving's rather explicit homicidal plot.

Finally, Gref changed his mind, and appeared before the Irvings. He particularly liked the Irvings' child. Gref would steal from the local townspeople and bring "gifts" to the family. He also liked to hitch rides into town on busses that passed by. One bus driver, annoyed by a mongoose on his roof, set an electric trap to capture Gref. But Gref precognated this—and avoided bus #82!

Gref's difficulties did not end there. Fearful of him, many townspeople planned to kill Gref, who stayed close to the Irving house for his own protection, throwing stones at people who came to call. Generous to a fault, Gref presented the family with so many rabbits that they began to supplement their income by selling them! When an occasional guest was allowed admittance to the Irving home, Gref would entertain the company by peeking through a hole in the ceiling and performing simple, amusing feats of precognition—such as calling heads or tails for repeated tosses of a coin.

Who was Gref? How could a mongoose speak so clearly? What are we to make of his self-definition as a ghost, a visitor from the fifth dimension? Unfortunately, these questions, like many others, are as yet unanswered. The mysterious powers of animals are only beginning to be understood. What we do know is that Gref can serve as an important clue in our search for the answer to the riddles of nature. When Gref was examined by naturalist and writer Ivan Sanderson it was discovered that the talking mongoose had three fingers and a thumb—not only unprecedented for a mongoose, but altogether singular in the animal kingdom.

Gref enjoyed riding busses. A famous American dog, called Owney, who touched deeply the human lives he entered was also a traveler—but Owney liked to ride the rails. Owney was a shaggy mongrel who became a mascot for clerks in the U.S. Post Office in Albany, New York, after he'd been found asleep behind mail-sacks. Owney enjoyed his new friends, but soon became restless and started accompanying the mail train shipments. The Albany postal workers realized that Owney couldn't be kept in one place. They let him wander, attaching a tag to his collar with a note asking clerks along the mail route to stamp the collar so that they might keep a record of Owney's travels. Soon Owney was known and welcome on mail cars across the country. But it didn't stop there.

On August 19, 1895, Owney was a stowaway on a mail ship bound for Japan. Meanwhile, word of this astounding adventurous dog had reached Japan. Arriving, Owney was honored by the Mikado. Yet even an imperial Japanese greeting did not satisfy Owney.

Soon he was on his way to China—and from there he kept on traveling around the world. When he returned to his good friends in Albany, his collar sagged with medals and mementos from all the lands and cities he'd visited. After Owney's death, a taxidermist gave him the final accolade of preparing him for permanent exhibition in the Smithsonian Institute, the national museum in Washington D.C.

Americans, of course, aren't alone in commemorating extraordinary dogs. If Owney had lived to visit Japan later on, he might have met a fiercely loyal canine named Hachi, who regularly saw his master off to work at a Tokyo railroad station, then met him on his return at five in the afternoon. One day, however, tragedy struck. Hachi's master didn't come back on the 5:00—he had died that day while at work.

Whether or not Hachi sensed that his master was dead, he never gave up hope. Every day for the next ten years Hachi was at the station in time to greet the 5:00, staring anxiously into the faces of detraining passengers. Then, he'd turn away sadly and trot home.

The people of Tokyo and eventually of all Japan learned of this and came to love Hachi.

When the dog died, the Japanese government erected a statue of Hachi on the spot where he had kept his ten-year vigil. Miniature replicas of the statue were cast in quantity and sent to all schools in the Japanese empire.

Another dog with an international flair to his astonishing character was a black-and-white Llewellyn Setter named Jim. Jim was owned by a man named Sam Van Arsdale in the town of Sedalia, Missouri. One day, when the dog was about three years old, Van Arsdale asked Jim to point out an elm tree. Jim trotted over to the nearest elm and put his paw on its trunk! Surprised and amused, Van Arsdale then asked Jim to indicate hickory, oak and walnut trees. Like a woodsman born, Jim had no trouble doing this.

When Jim was about eight years old, word of his unusual ability had finally circulated far enough to prompt some researchers from the University of Missouri's School of Education to come to Sedalia. The scientists were manifestly astounded by the setter's talent. By now, Jim was responding to commands in languages other than English. Jim, when asked in French to point out a specific license plate, could accomplish the task effortlessly. When commanded in German to single out a lady dressed in blue and to show his master a mustachioed gentleman and a child with long, blond hair, Jim happily complied, never answering incorrectly.

The experts from the university decided that the dog didn't really have a genetic comprehension of foreign languages. The only explanation—and this the researchers had to admit—was that Jim complied with the commands through the use of ESP.

Bill Schul, author of *The Psychic Power of Animals,* designed a valuable series of tests for one of the widest known and best documented psychic pets of recent times—a Boston Terrier named Missie, dubbed "The Psychic Dog of Denver." Missie was acclaimed by the London *Daily Mail* as one of our time's foremost prophets.

Missie was five years old before it was discovered that she was a psychic but even her birth was quite unusual. After having dropped a litter of three puppies, the mother began yelping in extreme pain. She was operated on, and the little pup who was to become a famous oracle was found lodged high in the ribcage.

Too small and weak to be kept with the rest of the litter, Missie was given to a retired floral designer named Miss Probert who had an innate sympathy for the pup—and all defenseless thing

As is often the case, Missie's extraordinary abilities were discovered quite by accident. Because most people don't suspect the awesome capacity of their pets, it is almost always up to the animal to step forward. How many more psychic pets would be discovered if people looked more actively for the signs of sixth sense in their pet? I'd venture to say thousands!

Anyhow, Missie's debut was reminiscent of how Rolf, the talking German Airedale, was discovered. Miss Probert was walking with Missie and they met a mother and child. The mother, anxious to show how sociable her little boy was, asked him to tell Miss Probert how old he was. The child remained silent—as children often will (and perhaps ought to!) when asked to perform.

The mother, answering for him, said the lad was three. Miss Probert, hoping to "bring the child out," leaned over him and said, "Three. Say three."

Instead of the child responding, Missie chimed in with three loud barks. Everyone laughed, and the child was probably relieved. Now, Miss Probert shifted her attention to Missie saying, "Okay. How old are you?" Missie answered with four barks. When her mistress asked how old she'd be *next* week, Missie barked five times.

Miss Probert had the good sense to know from that moment on that hers was no ordinary dog. She began paying close attention to Missie, asking her increasingly difficult questions. Unlike Rolf and Lola, Missie seemed to have worked out her own system for understanding and communicating numbers and letters.

As Miss Probert told Schul, "She developed her system entirely on her own. If a series of numbers were involved, such as a street address or phone number, she would bark so many times for the first number, pause, bark out the second number, pause, and so on. She coughed a strange little muffled sound for zero."

Missie's powers extended significantly further than anyone originally suspected. As she gradually revealed to the world just how many amazing things she was capable of, she astonished hundreds of people who came into contact with her. For instance, at social gatherings Missie entertained ladies by telling them how many coins they had in their purses, and could even guess exactly how many beans were contained in a sack. Her abilities in these matters seemed infallible.

Writing of Missie in *Psychic Magazine*, an author relates the story of one party at which Missie was asked to reveal the number of marks on playing cards held out of the dog's view. "This was," the writer reports, "the first time that Missie had ever been near a deck of cards, and yet she went through the entire deck without a mistake. Since nobody in the room saw the face of the card until after Missie had barked the response—at which time the experimenter showed the card to everyone—this would preclude the possibility of telepathy, making it a clear-cut case of clairvoyance."

Missie was always ready to astonish someone with her powers. She revealed to friends and strangers alike the exact dates of their birth. If that wasn't enough to send skeptics reeling, she would then proceed to bark out the exact serial numbers of the dollar bills they carried in their wallets. Once a local physician, who was absolutely cynical about the noted canine prophet, came to scoff at Missie and to prove to himself that the stories about the dog were untrue. Missie educated the good doctor about the secret world of animals by first revealing his unlisted home phone number and then telling him his Social Security card number. The doctor was convinced.

Missie's range of clairvoyance increased. In the presence of news reporters, she predicted the winner of the 1964 Presidential Election, as well as numerous other state and national contests. To verify the truthfulness of Missie's incredible performances of clairvoyance, Miss Probert made it a point to collect signed affidavits from the scores of men and women who had witnessed each prophecy.

Representative Dennis Gallagher of Colorado wrote that Missie "barked out correctly my Social Security number, the numerals in my phone number and address, and the number of letters in the street on which I live. She then gave my complete birth date—month and year. She responded without hesitation and Miss Probert gave her no clues of any sort. Miss Probert would not have known these mentioned numerals. As Shakespeare wrote, 'There are more things in heaven and earth, Horatio, than are dreamt of in your philosophy.' "

Missie predicted UFO sightings as well as the number of delays in the launching of Gemini 1. She was interviewed on radio station KLTN, in Denver, on New Year's Eve, 1965, and when asked when the New York City transit strike in effect then would end, she replied January 13—absolutely right! The next day she predicted, nine months before the fact, the outcome of the 1966 World Series.

Not only did she know which teams would play in the Series and which would win, but she also correctly foresaw the day the Series would end, and the score of the final game. On the international front, Missie predicted the date the Paris Peace Talks would begin, and when the Colorado National Reserve would return from Vietnam.

Missie's eventual passing was no less strange than her entire life. One day in May, 1966, Missie continually called Miss Probert's attention to the clock. Missie was a flawless teller of time. But now, whenever her mistress looked at the clock, barked out her signal for eight o'clock. Miss Probert, confused by the dog's insistence, would ask what the time on the clock was. Missie would bark out the correct time shown—but then would quickly and repeatedly follow with the signal for eight o'clock. Miss Probert later remembered that Missie repeated this seven times that day. At exactly eight o'clock, Missie died. She choked to death on a bit of her food. All efforts to revive the marvelous little dog failed.

Later, Miss Probert came upon a toy clock which had been given to Missie. It was lying in a corner of the room. The hands of the clock had been moved to read eight o'clock.

NINE

Horses, Birds, and other Pets Who Hold the Key

Most of the real-life dramas of precognition, clairvoyance, or psi-trailing of pets usually involve a dog or a cat. As I've pointed out earlier, this doesn't necessarily mean that our feline or canine companions have cornered the psychic market. Rather it reflects a close and observant relationship between human and dog or cat. Most creatures live too far from human society to learn how to bridge the communication gap. We have seen what a heroic effort it often takes for an animal to inform us of his psychic powers. Most of the psychic feats performed by, say, the fox, leopard or pelican are performed far from the scrutiny of civilization, so, for the most part, go unrecognized.

In the cases of animals who live close to humans but are not often observed performing acts of psychic power, I think the two operative elements here are expectation and affection. We do not expect our cattle, our pet flying squirrels, our box turtles to demonstrate intelligence, and certainly not extraordinary intelligence. And, of course, there is little question of affection, or love. I doubt that there have been significant cases in which the ingredient of love has been absent, of pets demonstrating psychic powers.

Another animal toward which humans traditionally have

directed great affection is the horse. In fact, horses have turned out to be incredibly surprising creatures. In the last chapter we described the typewriting clairvoyant horse, Lady Wonder. Yet one thing we can be sure of—for every recorded tale of psychic power in an animal, there are scores of unwritten tales. The horse, in particular, has a long, detailed, but essentially unrecorded psychic past. This is true, in part, because some of the closest relationships between horse and man have taken place outside of our civilized, everyday world—on the Great Plains, for example, or on battlefields—or have unfolded in rural privacy, where they go unnoticed by the press and scientists.

Many people who own horses don't spend enough time with them to truly understand the horse's character, or else the horse is viewed as a wholly utilitarian creature, meant to pull a plow or drag logs from the woods. Yet even with the apparent neglect of the horse's inner-life, there have been innumerable tales of riders' lives being saved by the precognition of the horse. In fact, the ability of horses to sense danger has become well-accepted. Even inexperienced riders will generally heed the horse's signals.

All of us have heard many true stories of horses stopping suddenly, just before their startled riders see a tree ahead drop a heavy limb in their path—or of horses who are whipped and forced to walk across bridges—moments before the bridge collapses. Even though many of us may be unaware of the psychic power of the animal kingdom, the wisdom and clairvoyance of the horse is generally respected.

The People's Almanac reports a fascinating case of a whole stable of remarkable horses that demonstrates not only the potential of equine intelligence but how one animal who takes a step beyond prescribed behavior can influence others of his species to take the same awesome step.

This stable of wizard horses was in Elberfeld, Germany. It is not altogether clear how the discovery was first made, but someone observed that one horse there named Mohammed had a knack for mathematics. Before long Mohammed was extracting cube roots—

not a simple task for human intelligence!

Mohammed gave his answers by tapping out the units with one front foot and then the other. If the answer was fifty-four, Mohammed would tap five times with his left foot and four times with his right. To make certain that no one was giving him visual clues, Mohammed often performed this feat with a sack tied over his head. But at the Elberfeld stables it did not stop with just one horse. Adding daily to human perception and appreciation of horses were Kluge Hans, (German for "Smart Jack"), and Zarif, who both could duplicate Mohammed's incredible skills.

Of course, there was always skepticism about these horses (it is, sadly, perhaps, part of the nature of humans to doubt immediately anything that is new or surprising). People could not shake the idea that the horses' trainer, a man named Karl Krall, was somehow cluing the horses by hand signals. When a totally blind stallion was added to the stables and demonstrated the same mathematical skills, cynical Germans were forced to admit that visual prompting was impossible, and that these horses were truly extraordinary!

From Hermitage, Tennessee, comes an example of the powers of another often under-estimated pet: the canary. The canary in question was one Bib, who lived with an elderly lady known as Aunt Tess. Her niece nightly checked to see if the lights were on in Tess's house. One harsh, rainy night the niece saw that the lights were on and assumed that all was well. She then drew her own curtains and settled down with her husband for the night.

Later, when the two of them were relaxing cosily before the fireplace, they became aware of an odd tapping at their window. At first, they assumed that it was a branch tapping on the glass. But it went on and on in a peculiarly persistent way. The tapping was accompanied by a high human cry.

Racing to the window, the niece pulled back the curtains. There was Bib, Aunt Tess's canary, who had been beating against the glass and chirping. The bird apparently had just expired, lay dead on the sill. Niece and husband were, of course, startled. Without quite knowing why, they raced over to Aunt Tess's.

They found the old lady in a pool of blood. She had fallen and had struck her head on the corner of a table. Because of Bib's heroism, Aunt Tess was saved.

Fate Magazine reports that a Reverend O.F. Robertson of Hartsville, Tennessee, had a seeing-eye *cow*. The cow in question—Mary—became aware that the Reverend's eyesight was failing. Robertson, almost totally blind, could barely find his way around his hilly farmlands. But Mary found a way to help her owner. Nudging him with her nose, she guided him perfectly over his land as he made his rounds. Before long, Mary, of her own volition, would accompany Robertson wherever he went.

We'll have more to say about simians later on but for now, in passing, let us mention an intriguing case reported in an Indian magazine called *The Burman*, brought to our attention by friends. With a babe in arms, a woman was walking along the shores of the Payaswami River, not far from New Delhi, when she accidentally dropped the baby. The infant fell into the water. The mother, who did not know how to swim, began screaming in anguish. Luckily, a group of monkeys was watching from a nearby tree. One brave monkey leaped into the river to rescue the child. With the baby safely placed at the mother's feet, the monkey scrambled back up its tree.

In recent years a new branch of biology has been developed, which combines the study of animal behavior, evolution, ecology, physiology and population into a field now called Sociobiology. Sociobiology attempts to explain the phenomenon of altruism. That is, it accepts the Darwinian theory that the struggle for existence is a matter of the survival of the fittest, but it also attempts to explain why the bonds of kinship and generosity continue to exist. In other words, if all of life is a struggle in which the strong overcome the weak, why is it that we find so many cases in which animals will struggle to save and protect a weaker being?

The most touching examples of animal altruism are those cases in which a member of one species nurtures a member of another—perhaps because it awakens our hope for the realization of the

Biblical promise that the lion shall dwell with the lamb. A version of Isaiah's dream was, in fact, enacted in the Osaka Zoo in Japan. Dr. Wada, the zoo's director, reported that an unexpected threesome was sharing a cage: a goat, a lion, and a sheep. The lion in the trio had been rejected by his mother, and his diet consisted primarily of vegetables and milk. He had become rather a favorite in the zoo. Dr. Wada, probably sensing an unusual gentleness in the beast, placed first a goat and then a sheep in with him. From Osaka, the report is that coexistence that resulted was not a wary truce, but perfect harmony. They not only ate and slept together, but enjoyed a play period that often began with the goat butting the lion.

The Texas professor and historian J. Frank Dobie, writing in *Nature Magazine*, recounts tales of close relationships between deer and dog, buffalo and mustang, fawn and kitten. Even so-called natural enemies can form unexpected relationships. Infant mice, orphaned, can find themselves being nursed by a cat. In England, there's been a case of a greyhound adopting a rabbit, although nightly he chased a mechanical rabbit that he would tear to pieces if he could catch it.

Sometimes, the love an animal feels for another can be an inspiration to act in a way outside its normal range of behavior. One Newark, New Jersey, dog named Mooch was a mascot for Fire Engine Company No. 11, but was notoriously afraid of fire and smoke. His phobia was a joke among the firemen. Though Mooch was a good companion in the station house he could never be coaxed to go near a fire—not even if it meant a ride on the fire truck!

One day, there was a serious blaze right near the station. It so happened that a female dog with whom Mooch was acquainted was trapped in the burning house. Mooch overcame his fear of flames and rushed into the inferno. Finding his female friend, he dragged the half-asphyxiated dog to safety. The men of Engine No. 11 awarded Mooch a medal commemorating his bravery, which the dog wore for the rest of his life.

You never know where you will find a wonderful story of animal bravery—like a superb true story in the *Reader's Digest*. A New

York City man named Eldon Bisbee had lost an aging French Poodle during a severe snowstorm. Bisbee looked everywhere for his frail friend. After a few hours he returned home, despondent. Too grief-stricken to sleep, he sat up through the night.

At three in the morning, his doorbell rang. It was a cab driver asking, "Are you the owner of a dog, a poodle?" The driver said he had the dog in his cab and had gotten Bisbee's address from the dog's collar.

While Bisbeee nursed the poodle, the cabbie warmed himself and told of the amazing circumstances behind the rescue. He had been cruising through the storm when a German Shepherd leaped into his path, planting himself before the headlights. The cabbie stopped, blew his horn, but the shepherd wouldn't budge an inch. When he rolled down his window to shout at the dog, the shepherd came over and began to whine. Still whining, the German Shepherd ran off a few feet into the snow, looking back so coaxingly that even the cabbie—a stranger to him—was induced to follow. The shepherd led the driver directly to the lost poodle, who lay almost completely buried in a snowbank. Apparently, she'd been hit and thrown there by a snowplow.

Perhaps the most stirring tales of bravery and precognition are those in which a human life is spared by an animal guardian. Surely, with all of the excellent reasons to attempt to communicate psychically with your pet we need not add that such communication can conceivably save your life—but the fact is that animals can and will sense danger far in advance of its actual manifestation.

Scientists in the People's Republic of China have learned that simple, open-minded observation of animal behavior can be instrumental in saving not just a few lives—but thousands of lives. In that vast, earthquake-vulnerable land there is a full-scale effort to understand ways in which creatures of the earth warn us of earthquakes. In an article in the January, 1977, issue of *Mother Jones*, a magazine not normally interested in psychic phenomena, John Harris describes the days preceding the massive Chinese quakes of 1976:

"...the reports of natural anomalies had reached a peak, and the several telephones at the Earthquake Office were kept busy all day. Some farmers reported that their chickens and geese would not enter their enclosures, others that their dogs were barking and running about. Cows in a dairy on the outskirts of Ying-k'on would not stay to be milked; in Haimoncheng Commune the water pump began to run without anyone's pumping it.

"Then, on the afternoon of February 3, a series of small tremors shook the ground...At 7:30 p.m. the sky was lit by flashes of lightning, there was a noise like thunder and the ground rolled with the motion of a strong earthquake. The reinforced brick houses of the commune crumbled to heaps of dusty rubble and the nearby city of Hai-ch'eng was leveled. But thanks to the timely order to evacuate and the prompt response to the order, three-quarters of the commune could report that there had been no fatalities."

There has been a great deal of pressure in the U.S. to use the proven abilities of animals to predict natural disasters, but so far not enough progress has been made. Frank Pross, president of the American Geophysical Union, tells us that "thousands of lives could be saved in Southern California if the state could learn from the methods of earthquake prediction in the People's Republic of China."

Significantly, some chimpanzees in an experimental lab in California's Stanford University were noted as displaying unusual behavior patterns two days before the great quakes rocked China— their predictive powers spanned those thousands of miles while our own technological attempts to devise an early-warning system have, to date, left us with little real protection.

The horrible earthquake which spread such devastation through Nicaragua was the setting for another tale of human lives being saved by the powers of an animal. Papers reported that a hundred and fifty youngsters were saved because they listened to the screaming warnings of their pet monkey, just moments before the orphanage in which they lived was demolished by the quake. The master of the orphanage, Father Petitto, was interviewed by the

National Enquirer, a news magazine with an audience of about twenty million and an interest in stories of psychic pets. Father Petitto said:

"I was in my room when I felt a slight tremor. The building shook slightly, but in Managua we have many tremors, and they do not mean anything. It was warm so I went into the garden for a stroll. We kept Chopa there in a cage. All the boys loved the sandy-haired monkey.

"Suddenly, Chopa started screaming. It startled me because she is usually very calm and quiet, particularly at night. I ran to her cage just when another slight tremor shook the earth. Chopa began screaming louder, rattling the bars on her cage. She had never behaved this way before. Suddenly a vision flashed across my mind. I remembered a time, as a boy in Italy, when I saw a donkey go crazy in the streets shortly before an earthquake. Could Chopa be trying to warn me that a severe earthquake was about to strike?

"I dashed inside the orphanage and ran upstairs where the boys were sleeping. I cried to them: 'Please, come quickly! Something terrible is about to happen.' I made them run into the garden in their underclothes. Then it happened. Just as the last boy was running from the orphanage, the whole building shook wildly—and fell apart."

In West Germany, Dr. Hans Bender, who has devoted his professional life to the study of psychic phenomena, has compiled and documented many hundreds of cases of animal ESP at Freiburg University's Institute for Parapsychology and Psychology. The cases documented at the Institute include the miles that went beserk in the streets of Skopje, Yugoslavia, as many as three days before the town was leveled by the earthquake of 1963 and the story of the gander who saved hundreds of civilian lives during World War II.

The setting for the tale of the psychic gander was at the Institute itself and the time was November 27, 1944. The Allies had launched an air attack against Freiburg, and the town's sirens were not functioning. Without doubt, the town's inhabitants would not have had a chance for survival had it not been for a very vocal gander who lived in Freiburg's main park.

The gander began squawking hysterically *hours* before the air raid, and continued to do so every fifteen minutes, driving hundreds of townspeople into air raid shelters. The gander himself was killed in the bombings, but the hundreds of survivors did not forget their web-footed benefactor. After the war, when the town was rebuilt and a new park was opened, a monument was erected to commemorate the gander who saved so many human lives.

One of my personal favorites is the verified story of a man named William H. Montgomery who set out to fish for flounder off the New England coast one day. He stocked his boat and called for his dog, a setter named Redsy. Redsy, since puppyhood, had always adored accompanying her master on fishing trips. But this fateful morning, Redsy did not respond to Montgomery's call. She absolutely refused to get in the boat.

Instead, she held her ground on the dock, barking at Montgomery, who increased the intensity of his commands while Redsy increased the intensity of her barking protests. The weather looked perfect and serene, there was scarcely a cloud in the sky. Already at sea, fifty other fishermen steered their boats toward the flounder banks. But Montgomery respected and trusted Redsy. He couldn't figure out the dog's strange behavior but something told him he'd better heed it. He decided to cancel the day's fishing trip.

Many of the boats that set out that day never made it back to shore. Not more than an hour after Redsy had warned Montgomery, an unprecedented storm rolled in from the sea and gale-like winds blew. Enormous waves, some measuring forty feet in height, crashed into boats and pummeled coastal cottages. More than six hundred human lives were lost. The storm was the great hurricane of 1938!

The *National Enquirer* reported this strange yet typical experience. A lady names Mary Kearns went on a camping trip with her Keeshund, Buffy. As Mrs. Kearns noted, "I already knew that

Buffy was somehow aware of certain things before they happened. At home, for example, he always seemed to know when my daughter was on her way to visit me—he'd bark and become excited and I knew she'd be at my door soon."

On the day of the camping trip, Mrs. Kearns chose a secluded spot in a valley, parked her car, and began to unpack. With each armload of supplies which she carried out of her car, Buffy ran up to her, barking with unnatural excitement—the dog seemed crazed, wild. There was no quieting him down. Mrs. Kearns decided that it would be easier for both her and Buffy if they'd simply pack their gear and find somewhere else to camp. She repacked the car and found another lovely camping spot on a hillside. Buffy was as calm as could be and slept the night.

"In the morning I broke camp," recalls Mrs. Kearns, and we started to travel again. Passing through town I bought a paper—and saw terrifying news. Three campers had been drowned in a flashflood that started with a heavy, unexpected rainstorm high in the mountains. I read further. Then I realized—the flood had raged down the very valley where I had intended to camp! There had been no warning about the possibility of a flood. No one had known it was coming. How had Buffy known there was something wrong with the campsite? I cannot answer—but I know that beyond doubt his psychic warning saved me from death."

The *Saturday Evening Post*, in choosing the "Ten Most Courageous Dogs of 1976," relates another impressive tale concerning a camping trip. The dog in question is named Zorro, a German Shepherd-wolf mixture owned by the Cooper family of Orangevale, California.

Zorro was awarded first place in the 1976 awards for saving his master, Mark Cooper, who'd been seriously injured in an eighty-five-foot fall into a ravine. Without hesitation, Zorro raced down the side of the mountain to get to his master's side. Cooper was struggling in Bullion Creek, in the ravine, and the last thing he remembered before losing consciousness was faithful Zorro, pulling him from the water. Then, while Cooper's backpacking companion went for help,

Zorro stayed with Cooper in the wilderness of the Sierra Nevada. He kept his master warm through a long cold night by lying on top of him.

Finally, as we continue in our re-definition of animal capacity and intelligence, let us relate three stories which involve prominent individuals. All three stories involve the prediction of death—an attribute of animal knowledge that the ancients were well aware of.

Schul, in his book *The Psychic Power of Animals*, relates that President Lincoln's assassination was predicted by his dog. He recounts the efforts of the White House aides to calm the dog down. "Suddenly," says Schul, "he went beserk! Although always quiet and docile, shortly before the tragedy the animal raced around the house in a frenzy, and kept up a dirge of unholy howling."

The next story tells of a dog owned by the renowned English novelist Thomas Hardy, author of *Jude The Obscure* and *Far From the Madding Crowd*. For thirteen years, Hardy's close companion was Wessex, a wire-haired terrier. Wessex, besides being loyal to Hardy, had an enormous fondness for a friend of Hardy's named William Watkins. Whenever Watkins appeared, Wessex would greet him with the great enthusiasm we all love in dogs. But one spring evening, Watkins appeared and the terrier greeted him with pitiful whines. Hardy thought the dog was sick or injured, but a careful examination revealed no physical problem.

Later, the dog joined the two men in Hardy's study. Throughout the evening, Wessex several times put his paw on Watkins's sleeve and then withdrew it, squealing and whining. Aside from his puzzlement over the dog's behavior, Watkins seemed in good spirits and perfectly healthy. The next morning, however, the telephone rang. Wessex usually barked at the phone's ring but this time he kept still and silent. He remained on the floor with his nose between his paws. The caller was Watkins's son. He was calling with the tragic news that his father had died suddenly—just an hour after leaving Hardy's home the night before.

Our final story in this chapter comes from Danton Walker, for many years a New York newspaper columnist covering the Broadway beat. It is a tale that sheds light on animals' ability to sense death approaching and it also adds new flavor to the cliché of rats abandoning a sinking ship. The story came to Danton Walker from the famous actor Raymond Massey.

Massey and his wife purchased a Manhattan town house in the East 80s. Across from their house was a rather large brownstone—a mansion, really—which was then unoccupied, but was soon rented by a socialite and her family. The socialite confided to Massey that she couldn't rid her house of the mice that infested it. A few days later, Mrs. Massey was astounded when she saw the mice evacuating from the brownstone. They appeared panic-stricken and disoriented. Several days later, the socially prominent tenant of the house committed suicide.

The mansion remained unoccupied for sometime, but then it was sold to a prominent businessman. One day while tending her house plants, Mrs. Massey again witnessed panicky hordes of mice streaming out of the brownstone across the street. A couple of days later, the businessman crashed his private plane into the Hudson River and was dead before rescuers could reach him.

Again, the mansion stood empty. But for everyone willing to believe in fate, there are at least a dozen more willing to ignore the unexplainable. An affluent playboy bought the house. Not long afterwards, his death was front page news. And, of course, once again the horrified Masseys witnessed the mass, frightened exodus of mice from that strange building on Manhattan's fashionable East Side.

PART FOUR

Animal Consciousness

At the Crossroads of Consciousness: Animals and the Ancients

I n attempting to understand the origin and nature of human life, men and women have devoted their lives to study of all the available evidence. We have hunted for ancient tombs and therein breathed the air of antiquity. We have built awesome magnifying lenses which can reveal distant thoroughfares of the solar system or the intricate knit of the oak leaf. We have studied the songs of poets long dead and peered at paintings inside caves. We have analyzed the soil, and scoured the ocean floor for relics and remains. On a universal scale, human history is brief, yet our origins remain enshrouded. We can scarcely picture our ancestors; imagining life as it was even a mere thousand years ago is an act of which, despite our vaunted sophistication, only a few humans are capable.

As we have implied throughout this book, one of the prime links between us as we are today and our past are the creatures with whom we still share the earth. Perhaps as you read these pages a pet is curled at your feet; that small animal can be an instrument of startling discovery.

Science, of course, has not ignored the vast animal resources in its attempts to explain and improve human life. Unfortunately, however, most of science's attention to animals has been focused on the physical metaphor—i.e., how modifications in the animal physiology can help us predict changes in our own. While some of this research has proved, and will continue to prove, valuable, it has also routed us into a dead-end in our understanding of animal life. It has led us to schoolrooms packed with students whose appreciation of animal life consists of mass dissections of insensate frogs.

While not all our scientists have backed away from understanding animals as emotional and psychological antecedants of humans, it is a field that, until now, has gone deplorably unexplored.

Part of the problem, of course, is connected to the social and political structure within which scientific experimentation must take place. In order to be awarded funds to study a problem, a researcher must submit a proposal and a design for the experiment. In competing with other scientists for scanty research dollars, a researcher has a better opportunity of being awarded a grant if he or she proposes to study how many times a rhesus monkey blinks under the influence of uncarbonated orange drink than if the proposal is to study the spiritual affinity between humans and felines.

We are like those overwrought heroes from novels who have scrambled up out of the "old neighborhood," and deny for the rest of their lives where they come from. Whereas once our society lived with full cognizance of the kinship between man and animal, the increasing complexity of worldly life has brought about a violent revulsion from our animal nature.

With the stratification of religious life and the hardening of class distinctions, animals have more and more been denied as our kin and become creatures either to be used or feared. Fairy tales about ravenous wolves and bears had a real and profound connection to the psyche. As *homo sapiens* gained increasing mastery over his environment, irrational and consuming fear of animals subsided, yet movement away from identification with animals continued unabated.

Imagine the horror of his contemporaries when Charles Darwin postulated that not only did we share the earth with the animal kingdom but that we ourselves were direct descendants of animals. This was an outrage to the religious orthodoxy of the time, and it was in direct contradiction to the prevailing intellectual fashions which favored strict rationality. How rational could men be if we had to share our family tree with orangutans?

Of course, when we speculate about what really took place at the dawn of human time, we are forced to contend with a massive insufficiency of hard evidence. But a recent and much heralded book written by Princeton's Julian Jaynes called *The Origin of Consciousness in the Breakdown of the Bicameral Mind* gives fuel to certain suppositions about the history of our psychic relations with the animal world.

Professor Jaynes describes the intellectual and physiological impact of human thought becoming rational, and discusses the creation of society and religion in terms of the evolution of our brains away from simple, divided, more animal-like structures into the complex, unified structures they are today.

As we struggled for our rational powers one can imagine how difficult it must have been to continue our unconscious identification with the animal world, and what the impact of these crucial changes was on our ability to psychically communicate with animals. As human nature evolved away from the animal world in order to master abstract thought it became confusing and even traumatic to still be in communication with nature, but to no longer be able to translate or digest that communication through the neocortex. And so these same animals who had once been brothers and sisters to primitive humans had to be placed in a new context— one in which they could be objectified. Jaynes tells us that when we read of men and women who hear voices telling them what to do, we are, in fact, getting an accurate description of how the primitive, divided mind worked. As this bicameral division became more difficult to cope with the voices were given names, monuments were erected to them, rituals devised in their honor.

It is, I think, highly suggestive of the relationship which once existed between us and the animal world, that the original deities worshipped were animal deities and then gods who mixed the attributes of animals and humans. In the following chapter, we will discuss fully the curious psychological alchemy of mixing humans with animals. For now let us examine briefly the spiritual history of our two most common household companions—the cat and the dog.

The Egyptians had a special understanding of and reverence for the cat. This appreciation for feline grace and intelligence was such that modern cat lovers still buy thousands of replicas of ancient Egyptian sculptures of cats—no people has ever been so successful in capturing the beauty and mystery of the cat as the Egyptians.

During the reign of the Egyptian kingdoms anyone seen killing or hurting a cat could be executed. One of the pivotal points in the Egyptian cosmology was Bast, a feline goddess who embodied the spirit of life and fruitfulness. Bast took more than one form. Sometimes she was represented as a lion-headed woman or a cat-headed goddess—in which form she was called Pasht. Though Bast/Pasht was considered even-tempered, she was also the goddess of war (just like our own cats who one moment may be purring in the sunlight and then very next dismembering a hapless moth). Actual animal representations of cats and other animal dieties were not only revered but at death were mummified like the highest royalty.

Bast was not the only animal deity worshipped by the Egyptians. There was Khnum, portrayed as a ram and one of the gods of creation. Thoth, a baboon, was the god of wisdom. (Thoth was also called Ibis.) Anubis, a jackal, was the god of the dead and Apis, a bull, was the guardian of tombs.

Another desert people, those of the Americas, who found intimations of a cosmic reality in the cat where the Mochican Indians of coastal Peru. The Mochicans, a remarkable people whose history remains vividly available to us through their beautiful pottery, had as their supreme god a feline deity called Ai apaec. Ai apaec was most often portrayed as a wrinkled old man with long cat fangs and whiskers. In the Mochican pottery, he is shown fulfilling the role of physician, farmer, and hunter. Ai apaec was also the god who watched over the act of copulation and insured that the union was fruitful. In every way, the Mochicans saw the cat as a beneficent creature—yet their brothers in the Andes, the Quechua Indians, saw the cat as a basically evil, fearful force.

There has always been a great division in human assessment of the cat. Probably no other animal on earth has maintained such a powerful hold on man's consciousness; no other animal has had fewer neutral things said about it. Cats have inspired awe, slavish affection; on the other hand, they have been feared, reviled, seen as the embodiment of all evil. Thousands upon thousands of cats have been slaughtered by people who did not trust them and who viewed the imperious aloofness of the cat as evidence of corruption.

In a volume entitled *The Book of Folklore*, we find a selection of some of the notions which the impenetrability of the cat has inspired in man:

Never kick a cat—you'll get rheumatism.
Never drown a cat—the devil will take revenge.
Cats have nine lives—but if you take one, the cat will haunt you.
Black cats bring bad luck.
It's good luck to own a cat.
Black cats are the helpers of witches.
Cats are powerful allies of workers of voodoo.
Cats' eyes are powerful ingredients in voodoo "wishing" potions.
Cats can see ghosts.
If a cat washes its face, it's a sign of rain.
A cat washing his face in the parlor means guests are coming.
A cat looking out of the window means rain.
A cat's pupils are nearly closed at low tide, wide open at high tide.
It's good luck to sleep with a cat.
Cats will suck the breath out of sleepers.
If a cat jumps over a corpse the deceased will become a vampire if the cat is not caught and killed.
Cats are devils and must be burned on Shrove Tuesday and Easter.
In Transylvania, a fertility rite involved bringing a cat to the home of newlyweds and putting it into a cradle and rocking it.

As we mentioned before, the cat has generally been viewed as the most psychic of all animals, the creature most adept at occupying simultaneously the physical and the spirit world. Appallingly often, however, the subtlety and mysteriousness of the cat, combined with its often manifest psychic powers, have inspired a fear so pervasive that the outcome has been wild, incredible violence. Cats are still often subject to the savage whims of humans, yet in the Middle Ages, with its irrational and limitless dread of witchcraft and all forms of spirituality not officially sanctioned by Church or State, the killing of cats was commonplace. Cats were often put to death in mass executions, burned in enormous bonfires. When women who were accused of witchcraft were tortured and burned, their cats, thought to be consorting with the witches were also destroyed.

A text on *Cats and People* gives a vivid and horrifying picture of the war against feline intelligence. "Christians burned cats in, or slowly roasted them over Lenten fires everywhere in Europe," reports the author of that work. "They stuffed them into wicker baskets and threw the baskets into the fire; when Elizabeth was crowned in England, such a basket of screaming cats was immolated as a warning to the underworld and an amusement to the godly.

"Louis XIV of France danced gaily around a fire with his nobles and their ladies in 1648, their ears filled with the horrible screams of dying cats. In Scotland they burned innumerable cats at a celebration known as Taigheirn which lasted four days. There the cats were dedicated to the devils—which is to say the ancient gods they served—and then roasted slowly."

This violent dichotomy between reverence and villification has not plagued the dog as much. While many people's have worshipped canine gods, there hasn't been the radical reaction against this ancient allegiance, no reign of terror unleashed against the dog—even though the dog, and his cousin the wolf, have represented in human consciousness fearful aspects of our own character.

Indeed, the man with too much wolf in him has been a standby in the popular imagination of horror; and the wolf itself to this day continues to be wantonly hunted, tracked down and destroyed with a vengeance that far exceeds any danger inherent in the wolf itself.

In ancient Egypt there was a sect devoted to the worship of wolves. Their center was Lycopolis, and among other practices these ancient Egyptians imitated the natural habits of their venerated wolves by ritually eating sheep. The Greeks considered Apollo a wolf god, and the Arcadians worshipped Zeus as a wolf-god. Yet even the wolf worshippers lived in fear of what the wolf aspects of human beings meant to our sense of character and morality. From the beginning we sensed the kinship between ourselves and the animal kingdoms and from the beginning—even as we worshipped and celebrated animals—we recoiled from too close an identification.

For example, the Arcadians had a festival for their wolfish Zeus every nine years. At this festival a boy was sacrificed and his entrails were mixed with the innards of slaughtered sheep and goats. This gruesome stew was served up to the shepherds. Whoever was so unlucky to eat the human items in this appalling mess would be turned into a wolf, remaining one for nine years. His only chance to become human again was to spend those years steadfastly resisting the desire to eat human flesh.

We can see in this practice the ambivalence with which we view animals, a mixture of admiration and dread which comes perhaps from our age-old efforts to fully distinguish ourselves from our animal ancestors. This dread of the animal within us has its most vivid expression in the various tales of men who are turned into wolves, and other generally horrific stories of decent God-fearing humans being transformed into lawless, lustful beasts.

A psychiatrist might recognize this terror as a fear of the Id, that untamed part of each of us which exists quite independent of the rules of culture and society. This terror we have of our unexplored selves has, more than any other single factor, I think, served to separate us from animals and has deadened our sensitivity to them.

Patricia Dale-Green, in her brilliant and erudite *Love of the Dog*, illuminates hundreds of aspects of the spiritual relationship between humans and dogs. From her book we can trace the dog as deity through the Greco-Roman period in Egypt, where Hermanubis was the dog god. She writes: "Priests of Hermanubis wore wooden dog-masks with black muzzles and ears and wide black stripes drawn across the neck, and they usually carried the herald's staff. "It is recorded that in Rome . . . a man who wished to leave the city unrecognized borrowed a dog-mask from a friend . . . and made his way through the streets mimicking those celebrating the mysteries of the god."

Later, Gnostic sects mixed Christianity with the older rites, and many Gnostics identified the figures of Hermanubis with the representations of Christ. As Dale-Green points out, "Gnostic gems show the dog-god with is arms outstretched in the form of a cross: a graffito scratched on a wall of a Roman house showed a dog-headed man holding a cross, with someone standing in front worshipping him . . . Throughout the cult of Hermanubis, dogs were venerated (but were never considered to be divine as were cats), and the city of Cynopolis was the center of the dog cult. Here dogs were ritually fed on food provided free by city inhabitants. When a dog died a natural death, members of the household shaved their heads and bodies (when a cat died they shaved only their eyebrows!) and threw away any food present in the house at the time of its death."

The Hindus also worship a dog-god in the form of Bhairava, who is one of the more frightening aspects of the great Hindu deity Siva. The Chinese Buddhists incorporated the dog into their cosmology in a curious way. In India, the lion was the supreme symbol of Buddhism, but when Buddhism came to China most Chinese had no knowledge of lions. It was noticed, however, that the Imperial dog of Peking—the Pekinese—somewhat resembled the Indian drawings of lions and with that inspiration the Chinese created the now famous lion-dog, an image which still proliferates from Tibet to American antique shops.

Speaking of Tibet, Patricia Dale-Green has some fascinating insights into the spiritual lives of some currently popular breeds.

"In ancient times Tibetan spaniels were so highly prized that they formed part of the tribute annually paid to the Emperors of China by the successive ruling dynasties at Lhasa. That is how the breed originally became established in China. They were treasured as pets in oriental courts and are portrayed in early Chinese paintings, tapestries and ceramics. The whole court went into mourning when one of these little dogs died ... In Tibet today these dogs are rarely found outside the monasteries. As sacred animals, they are closely guarded, and the monks will never part with a bitch. People owning them in this country say that they make characteristic movements with their paws, as if they were still turning prayer wheels....

"Another sacred Tibetan dog is the Apso—so called because of its resemblance to the small, long-haired, indigenous goat ('apso' being a corruption of 'rapso,' the Tibetan word for 'goat'). From very early times Apsos were bred in Tibetan monasteries and also in the palace of the Dalai Lama. It is said that the souls of lamas who had not been as good as they should have been enter the bodies of Apsos at death...."

Tribal deities were often canine. In South America there was wide-spread belief among certain tribes that human life was first released from the Underworld by a dog scratching up at the earth. When the Incan armies conquered Peru (before they themselves were conquered by the Spanish) they found in the Temple of Huanca a figure of a dog kept as the highest deity. The Kalangs, a tribe of North Borneo, have worshipped a red dog, and each family kept a wooden image of the dog in their house. They prayed to this dog and burned the wooden image a thousand days after anyone close to them died. At marriage ceremonies, the body of the bride and the bridegroom were rubbed with the ashes of a red dog's bones.

Dogs have also been curiously linked with the practice of medicine, especially in those times when the medical and spiritual arts often intertwined. There is even a special term—cynotherapy, which means "the practice of healing by means of dogs." According to Dale-Green in *The Cult of the Dog*, "There are four different ways in which the dog has been connected with healing: its image was common to the iconography of many divine physicians... it appeared to heal many people by licking their injuries; parts of its body were used in folk medicines, and its blood was used to exorcise demons of disease."

Some aspects of cynotherapy seem well-rooted in provable facts. The tongue of a dog, for instance, *does* seem to have healing powers, at least in terms of the infections to which dogs are vulnerable, and it is not unreasonable that many have believed the touch of the dog's tongue to be purifying. Other aspects of dog-related healing are less easily understood. For instance, a dog's head burnt to ashes has been used to treat rectal diseases, sores, burns, and syphilis. Blind puppies have been eaten as a care for summer sores, and the flesh of a suckling pup has been mixed with myrrh and wine in the treatment of epilepsy.

Just as the supernatural powers ascribed to cats eventually resulted in a reaction *against* felines, dogs too have paid for their close relationship with humans through countless sacrifices and wanton slaughters. The Iroquois used to sacrifice dogs ritually in order to send them on their way as messengers to the Great Spirit. In Greenland, when a child died he or she would be buried with the head of a dog so the child would have a trustworthy guide to heaven.

The Mexicans and Peruvians also killed dogs so they might guide deceased humans to the next world, and more often than not these sacrifices were brutal. The belief in the goodness of dogs has led many to be killed in exorcism rites, especially in China, where it was believed that a screeching, bleeding dog frightened off evil spirits.

Dogs have also been used to absorb sickness and bad luck. In Jamaica, hairless dogs called "fever dogs" were placed across humans to take away fever. In Oldenburg, a person suffering from fever would treat the illness by placing a bowl of sweet milk before a dog and reciting the following chant: "Good luck, you hound. May you be sick and I be sound." And in Brittany, there were elaborate priestly rites in which black dogs were given possession of wicked souls and then ritually destroyed.

Although the spiritualization of the dog never had the

psychological backlash as the deification of the cat even as the dog fell from grace it remained essentially friendly to mankind, there is no mistaking the gradual degeneration of the broad human perception of all animals, including the so-called "man's best friend." Negative imagery regarding the dog began to accumulate and before long the canine form represented humans' sense of danger and damnation more than it represented innocence or blessedness.

Moses is said to have regarded the dog as unclean, and Mohammedans believed that a water vessel that had been used by a dog must be ritually scrubbed seven times and scrubbed with earth. (A far cry from the belief that the licking of a dog can heal wounds!) Similarly, the Hindus believed that a dog walking between pupil and master rendered the day's work useless.

Naturally the scourge of rabies contributed to the fear—and hence the hatred—of dogs, especially in the Middle Ages when rabies was associated with Plague. Yet there really isn't any rational explanation of the growing contempt for the dog. If these notions were based on principles of hygiene, then why was it accompanied by a systematic divorce from all the other animals as well? Clearly, as in the case of the cat, the turning against the dog was a part of our unacceptance and terror of our own animal natures.

And so, with Europe falling beneath a shadow of fear, generated from without by the crumbling of the old classical order, and from within by the leaps of human consciousness, new folk beliefs about the dog emerged, generally of a terrifying nature. For instance, Latvian folk tales postulated the edge of the world where horendous dog-men lived. These dog-men sometimes had a human body and a canine head (with a Cyclopean eye) and sometimes they were said to be half man-half dog, divided vertically—straight down the middle!

Like the cat, though not as much so, the dog-man came to be viewed as a partner of those who practiced "black magic." Scottish superstition postulated that witches regularly worshipped a small black dog perched on a rock, and a Frenchman of the Middle Ages claimed to have attended a witches' meeting and seen the Devil—in the form of a large black dog. Freemasons, the theological scourge of the Christian era, were as a matter of course believed to have sold their souls to the Devil and the Devil attended their notorious meetings in the form of a black poodle, whose backside the Freemasons were alleged to kiss. In Goethe's classic *Faust*, Mephistopheles also appeared in the form of a black poodle. For those who have known and loved poodles, it is difficult to take with the appropriate seriousness these immortal lines from the great German poet:

> In length and breadth how doth my poodle grow.
> With bristling hair now doth the creature swell
> Huge as a hippopotamus
> With fiery eye, terrific tooth,
> Ah! now I know thee, sure enough!
> Cease thus to gnash
> Thy ravenous fangs at me! I loathe thee.

To be sure, the Christian era didn't signal a uniform turning away from human identification with animals—or at least it did not usher in a time in which everyone feared animals and animal nature. Though the association between the more "primitive" religions and animal worship meant that as monotheism struggled for its world-wide hegemony, a certain built-in, even official hostility toward the animal kingdom was all but inevitable. Still, an affection for animals continued to survive. St. Francis of Assisi's love of animals is a good example of love seen as a pathway toward God. In certain pictures, St. Christopher is depicted with a dog's head.

However, on the whole, animals were feared, just as we have learned more and more to fear the "animal" inside us. The animal world prowled the nights of Europe and Asia, just as the animal nature of humankind prowled the more private nights of the mind. Seeking redemption, but painfully conscious of his own un-worthiness, medieval and modern man could only become uncomfortable with those creatures who seemed to embody all that religious teachings said was impure. Francis Thompson, in his brilliant poem "The Hound of Heaven," captures this terror forever as he describes the flight from The Hound:

I fled Him, down the nights and down the days;
I fled Him, down the arches of the years;
I fled Him, down the labyrinthine ways
Of my own mind....

ELEVEN

Lycanthropy: The Possession and Transformation of Humans Into Animals

Even a casual study of history reveals that humans have had, from the beginning, a powerful relationship with the animal world. Starting with our own animal ancestry and proceeding to the first organized hunt (in which humans literally chased, slew, and ate their own forebears), the animals of the earth have inspired in men and women feelings of kinship and awe as well as revulsion and terror. As I have attempted to stress throughout *Psychic Pets*, the permanent and inescapable connection between human and animal is a bedrock truth of our existence. Acceptance of this truth can well lead to our having a heightened sense of our own reality, as well as giving us an opportunity to be reunited with aspects of our own nature from which we have, over the ages, drifted away.

In the preceding chapter I discussed how animals have figured in our attempt to find spiritual justification for life on earth. I mentioned animal sacrifices as well as animal gods, but in this chapter I'd like to touch upon one of the most extraordinary aspects in the relationship between human and animal: possession and transformation.

It is more than obvious that the phenomenon of a human being transforming himself or being transformed into an animal is an astonishing occurrence. If such transformations actually can take place there is, as far as I know, no plausible explanation of how. Yet, whether or not certain humans actually can assume a cat or wolf or other animal form is of secondary importance here. What is most interesting about the phenomenon of transformation is its widespread belief over many, many years.

The true significance of the legends of werewolves is what they reveal about the profound and often perplexing relationship between the animal kingdom and man's animal self.

In all probability, tales of animal transformation were among the very first ever told. If they were true, they were among the first investigations of our place in the general design of life. If they were fanciful, they perhaps represent the birth of human imagination. At the original stages of human awareness, little if any distinction was made between human and animal life. Sometimes, this ubiquitous sense of creation even included inanimate objects. Humans in the "savage" state credited animals with an intelligence equal and similar to their own. More importantly, there was no strict line of demarcation between human and animal nature. Far more clearly than we do now, primitive humans lived with an insight that all of existence is inextricably linked. This perception of the "one-ness" of creation led quite naturally to a belief in the *impermanence* of outward forms—a belief which was the basis for the extensive folklore concerning transformations of humans into animals or animals into humans.

The towering spiritual document of the Hindu East, the *Bhagavad Gita*, suggests that "Wise people see the same soul in the Brahman, in worms and in insects, in the dog and the elephants, in beasts, cows, gadflies, and gnats." Sir James George Frazer's *The Golden Bough* tells us that the Cherokee Indians used their perception of the impermanence of distinction between human and animal as a way of evoking the powers of animals in time of need.

A Cherokee, beginning a long winter journey, prepared for the ordeal by singing and dancing certain rituals designed to summon the spirits of the wolf, fox, oppossum, or any other wild animal whose feet were immune to frostbite. The words of the ritual chant were, "I become a real wolf, a real deer, a real fox, and a real opposum." At that, the traveler would give a long howl or would bark like a fox and scratch at the ground. And then, emboldened by this rite of homeopathic magic, the journey would begin.

While the stories of human-into-animal transformations have their origins in an ancient system of belief which saw all the world as one, the tales of possession and transformation most familiar to us are ones imbued with terror, horror, and death. This change is quite in keeping with the shift in the human attitude toward the animal world which I discussed in the preceding chapter. Once, humans identified positively with their own animal natures, but as societies became more organized, this once joyous sense of kinship was struck with a kind of dread.

When a modern woman or man thinks about a human assuming animal form, he or she is not likely to visualize a Cherokee brave evoking the powers of the fox in order to make a long winter's journey. Rather, transformations have come to mean a kind of demonic possession, an overwhelming of the human soul and conscience by a base and uncontrollable animal force. If transformation means anything to most people it means werewolves—men turned into shaggy, bloodthirsty beasts who must be destroyed.

The tales of transformations tell of far more than werewolves, however. There are stories of were-vixen, were-foxes, lion-men, tiger-men, human serpents, bird-women, swan-maids, ancestor-bears, and countless other manifestations which have found their way into folklore, mythology, religion, and the annals of law.

In the Middle Ages particularly, powers of transformation were pursued and were viewed by many as an occult privilege, a kind of spiritual alchemy. As time passed, however, the stories of transformations came to be viewed almost exclusively as symptoms of evil and the motives of anyone who wished to take animal form were looked upon with a suspicion that often led to outright hatred. The accusations of greed, cruelty, cannibalism (often an unconscious metaphor for lust) and lust itself were brought against those suspected of taking animal form. The medieval period saw countless trials—some grand and formal, others spontaneous and savage—

for the supposed crime of *lycanthropy*.

Lycanthropy is the technical term given to the condition of a man who believes he has become an animal, or for someone who is accused by others of desiring such a transformation. Literally, the word means wolf-man, the wolf standing in the European mind for the mystery and malevolence of the wilderness. However, lycanthropy would also describe transformations into tigers, hyenas, or any other wild animal.

A woman writing under the name of Frank Hamel has supplied us with an extremely complete and useful guide to human/animal transformations in her book *Human Animals*. In discussing the causes of transformations, Hamel lists several of the most commonly cited: "contact with a were-animal, touching what he has touched, wearing an animal skin, rubbing the body with ointment, slipping on a girdle, buckling on a strap..."

This partial list of causes divides itself between inadvertent transformations and those which are clearly willed. This division reflects the split in the attitude toward lycanthropy. In some cases, those who were believed to have been transformed into animals were suspected of practicing black magic while others were believed to have been cast into animal form against their will. However, even those who became were-animals without wanting to did not escape condemnation. In such cases, involuntary transformation into animal form was considered a crime—either moral or physical—and was looked upon as judgment from above.

People as a matter of course retained a certain watchfulness for the symptoms of lycanthropy. The signs of someone evolving (or devolving) into the were-animal state were extreme restlessness, as well as anxiety, and then the spontaneous or gradual adoption of the traits of a certain animal.

As the lycanthropy continued, the were-animal was thought to experience an uncanny increase in strength and endurance. Since most were-animals were accused of transforming into carnivorous animals, it was also suspected that blood-lust increased as the lycanthropy progressed. Finally, the body of the were-animal would change into the specific animal shape, and the man or woman would roam the wild with beast-like cohorts.

Pre-destination to were-animalism was often noticed in the appearance of a man or woman. Certain physical peculiarities, along with anything amiss in the psychological make-up, would insure someone a lifetime of being regarded with suspicion. For instance, if your eyebrows had a tendency to grow together you were considered a potential were-animal. Women with facial hair were also likely to be viewed with a certain fearful expectation.

Naturally, the dread of the animal instinct and power which led to the hatred and fear of lycanthropy also inspired some to desire transformation. Just as some have used the Catholic Church's condemnation of evil as justification for the Black Mass, some people turned the fear of the were-animal upside down and professed a desire to assume animal shape. It was considered to be everything, from a relaxing pastime to a form of heightened consciousness, and while most of society endeavored to protect itself from the were-animal there were others who strove to perfect sure-fire methods of transformation.

Those who were accused of such practices were handled with particular harshness. They were assumed to be in the Devil's service. Sorcery, of course, was for a while in direct competition with the established Church and was a prime heresy. Sorcerers who aided in the creation of were-animals were brought to "trial" by the hundreds, and were almost invariably convicted. Then they were either burned alive or broken on the wheel.

No society is free from outbreaks of hysteria. In the United States today is a thoroughgoing fear of the misfit, who translates his inability to adapt to society into murderous rage, the sexually starved or twisted individual who attacks children, the delusionary who becomes a mass slayer. All of these psychiatric phantoms can with one outburst hold millions riveted in fear. Only recently, for example, in New York a killer calling himself Son of Sam commanded the total attention of the most sophisticated city in the world. (Curiously, the man confessing to Son of Sam's crimes said that he got his orders to kill through his dog—a significant detail which connects this one particular villain to the villains of old.)

People in the Middle Ages also lived in fear of the deviant and the were-animal was one of this fear's most extreme manifestations. What today might be called homosexuality, transvestism, or even child molestation was explained through sorcery, possession, and transformation. Compare, for example, any recent tragedy involving a sexual assault on a child and this account of the 1573 trial of a Frenchman named Giles Garnier, who was arrested for devouring several children while in the form of a were-wolf.

Garnier was accused of seizing a young girl in a vineyard, killing her and dragging her into the woods where he tore the flesh from her bones using claw and tooth in wolf-like fashion. He was said to have found this human flesh so delectable that he brought some home to his wife so she might share it with him. A week after the feast of All Saints, Garnier captured yet another ten- or twelve-year-old girl and was about to devour her when someone happened on the scene and Garnier took flight.

A week later, still in wolf-form, he killed and ate a young boy. He was also accused of falling upon a boy of twelve or thirteen and carrying him into the woods—this was to have taken place while Garnier was in human form. What made this act particularly outrageous was that Garnier was supposed to have been ready to cannibalize the young boy even though it was a Friday! However, this act was interrupted by some strangers who happened by and caught Garnier before the slain boy could be eaten.

The captured man admitted to his crimes. He was placed on trial and the judge pronounced sentence: "The condemned man is to be dragged to the place of execution and there burnt alive and his body reduced to ashes." The trial took place in January of 1573 and the account of it was accompanied by a statement from Daniel d'Ange, directed to the Dean of the Church of Sens.

D'Ange wrote:

"Giles Garnier, lycophile, as I may call him, lived the life of a hermit, but has since taken a wife, and having no means of support for his family fell into the way, as is natural to the defiant and desperate people of rude habits, of wandering into the woods and wild places. In this state he was met by a phantom in the shape of a man, who told him that he could perform miracles, among other things declaring that he would teach him how to change at will into a wolf, lion, or leopard, and because the wolf is more familiar in this country than the other kinds of wild beasts, he chose to disguise himself in that shape, which he did, using a salve with which he rubbed himself for this purpose, as he has since confessed before dying, after recogizing the evil of his ways."

The capture and execution of Garnier had tremendous impact on the people of Dole, Garnier's village. The dread of were-wolves and such creatures was always ready to explode into a full-fledged obsession and after the *affaire* Garnier, a decree was issued which granted the people of Dole the right to "assemble with javelins, pikes, arquebuses and clubs to hunt and pursue the were-wolf and to take, bind, and kill it without incurring the usual fine or penalty for indulging in the chase without permission."

Tales of transformation seem to occur in all folklore throughout the world. Most of them are tales of origins, expressing some ancient understanding of evolution as well as a holistic appreciation of the kinship between all living things. The Turtle Clan of the Iroquois, for example, thought themselves descendants of a great turtle who one day shed his shell and developed into a human. The Choctaws postulated that at one time they lived underground as crayfish and the Miri said they were ancestors of a large deer. The Ojibways believed their antecedents were a pair of cranes who settled on Lake Superior to be transformed by the Great Spirit into a man and a woman. The Osages said they were the product of a most unlikely mating—between a snail and a beaver. According to their tales, the snail burst its shell and sprouted legs and arms and became a handsome man who wed a "beaver maiden."

In West Africa, as well as many other places, it was commonly believed that humans had four souls, one of which was called the "bush-soul." This bush-soul lived in an animal in the wild. If this carrier of the bush-soul was shot or trapped, the human whose soul he carried would also die. Bush-souls were regarded as hereditary. Sons inherited them from their father, and by daughters from their mother. Closely related to this belief was the belief that humans could and did change into the animal who carried his or her soul. In Iceland, for example, it was believed that family members had an animal other, called fylgia. Fylgia took the form of a dog or a bird and was routinely considered a double of the person it represented.

What is so particularly interesting about the tales of transformation told by uncivilized peoples is that they are generally cheerful, and free of the dread and hatred that came to characterize the European version. The ancient folk beliefs about animals originated in a time when humans still accepted and appreciated animal nature, both in the wild and in themselves and represent a lost consciousness, a lost consciousness which the European mind attempted to bury and which only recently is being rediscovered.

It would be wrong, however, to suppose that the fear of animal nature was something invented by the church in the Middle Ages. Pliny the Elder, the Greek historian, tells of were-wolves who feast on human flesh, and the familiar expression "turncoat" is in fact a translation of the Latin word *versipelles*, a synonym for were-wolf.

The were-fox is also the subject of many tales and reports. In Japan, stories of were-foxes are most common because the Japanese regarded the fox as more skillful than any other animal in assuming human form. What distinguishes the Japanese legends of the were-fox are most common because the Japanese regarded the fox as more skillful than any other animal in assuming human form. What distinguishes the Japanese legends of the were-fox from our more familiar tales of the were-wolf is that the transformation is generally from beast to human. Also, the stories tend to be far less sinister.

One tale of the were-fox recounts the story of Ono, who spent years looking for his ideal of feminine loveliness. He met her on a moor and instantly married her, and soon after that she delivered to him a child. Simultaneous with the birth of their son, Ono's dog had a pup who became incurably antagonistic to Ono's wife. She beseeched him to destroy the dog, but he didn't. One day the dog attacked her so violently that she panicked and took on her fox-form, and fled. Ono called after her: "You may be a fox, but you are the mother of my son, and I love you. Come back when you please, you will always be welcome." And every evening she crept back and slept in Ono's arms.

According to Frank Hamel in *Human Animals*, "The were-fox has a strange manner of bringing about transformation. Roaming over a grassy plain, the animal picks up a skull, puts it on his head, and facing toward the north star, worships silently. At first he performs his religious genuflections and obeisances slowly and circumspectly, but by and by his motions become compulsively rapid and his leaps wondrously active. Yet, however high he jumps toward the stars, he endeavors to keep his skull crown immovable, and if after a hundred acts of worship he succeeds, he becomes capable of transforming himself into a human being."

The idea of one's lover being in actuality a transformed creature of the wild seemed to have been a curious idea in the Orient but not one to cause any great displeasure. In the East, unlike in Europe, the mysteries of life and sexuality and the fate accorded to women who take animal form were accepted with a certain openness of spirit.

In Europe and America, the power to transform oneself into an animal was considered a proof of witchery. If the fear of witches can be said to stand for a kind of sexual hysteria which takes the form of hating women, then it is curious indeed to note how various were the animals into which women were accused of turning themselves. In the Middle Ages, witches were forced to confess to the crimes of turning themselves into cats, dogs, horses, and hares and to have been given such powers by the Devil himself. Indeed, even the modern conception of a witch would not be complete without a cat or two (preferably black) thrown into the picture. The concept of hag and cat has been reduced to a kind of spoofery in our own day—

though the fear and mistrust millions today have of cats certainly is related to the old stories of witchery.

Sometimes an animal has been accused of doing the Devil's bidding, without the animal being traced back to a particular human form. In 1474, in the town of Basle, a cock was put on trial for having laid an egg! After a lengthy investigation, the cock was sentenced to death—not as a cock but as a sorcerer. The cock, in fact, was burned at the stake, the execution taking place with the strictest rituals of justice. Such trials were by no means everyday events, but ninety-two legal proceedings were brought against animals in the French Courts between the years 1120 and 1740!

One other notable animal trial took place in Lavegny, in 1457. The defendants this time were a sow and her six piglets. They were tried for the murder of a young girl who had been found partially eaten. The sow was judged guilty and sentenced to death. But her litter of piglets were finally acquitted. The reason? They were young and under the spell of their evil mother. It was generally believed that witches and black magicians had "familiars," which were animals who stood by them and obeyed their commands, carrying the malignancy of the godless human far and wide.

PART FIVE

Animals at the Frontier of Science

TWELVE

Science and the Psychic Pet

Our understanding of animals has always been caught between the rational and the irrational. When human thought and belief was at its least rational—when magic was believed to be unquestionably true and our actions seemed governed by a thousand unknown spirits—human sympathy and insight into animal nature was in some respects at its highest point. However, as we struggled to control our own irrational impulses and make our way of life more orderly, the common view of animals became more and more distorted and irrational.

The impulse toward rationalism turned humans against a part of themselves—a part that came to be thought of as "base" or "animal" nature. This hatred of the part of ourselves that couldn't be tamed or perfected led to a number of disorders—among them, a fearful, sometimes cruel, and always distorted view of animals. In that way, the increasing rationality of the Western mind led to an increasingly *irrational* view of animals.

In our attempt to better understand our relationship with animals we must certainly regain the openness and the desire to. communicate which marked human thought at its earliest stages. But there is, quite obviously, no chance that we are going to reverse time and culture and suddenly become like our distant forebears.

We live in a scientific age. Science has, from its inception, concerned itself with the study of animal life. Experiments using animal subjects form the backbone of an enormous amount of psychological and medical research, both in the laboratory and in the wild. Science has given little encouragement until recently to those who suspected that our relations with animals had become severely and tragically limited. To those who claimed that animals possessed powers of insight, response, and precognition that extended far beyond the boundaries of instinct, science either answered with dismissive scorn or failed to respond at all.

Today, the study of psychic powers in animals is, at long last, gaining some influential adherents within the scientific community. From the United States Army to Duke University to the USSR's University of Leningrad, researchers and theorists are studying cats, dogs, and hundreds of other animals in order to determine how ESP and other psychic abilities work. In the Soviet Union, the study of what is loosely called parapsychology has gained a great deal of official support. Research into ESP and other psychic phenomena has received more generous funding and wider respect there than anywhere else. This is rather ironic since the Soviets consider themselves the world center for the philosophy of materialism and have always been actively unfriendly to spiritual philosophies.

There have been isolated scientists who have wondered whether or not animals possess powers beyond those official science acknowledges. But an officially credited, long-term study of this subject wasn't begun until Duke University inaugurated its study in the Parapsychology Lab about thirty years ago. When it was first decided to begin studying psychic power in animals, the field of investigation was limited to three distinct types of animal behavior: pets who traced their masters over long distances and found them in totally unfamiliar locations; the uncanny flight of homing pigeons who are released in strange territories without previous flight training; and cat behavior in enforced-choice experiments conducted without sensory clues.

One of the first experiments conducted at Duke was supervised by Dr. Karlis Osis. Dr. Osis's intention was to see if psychic communication could take place between animals and humans. Six kittens, ranging in age from five to eight months, were used as the initial subjects. Before beginning the experiments, Dr. Osis attempted to build a sense of trust and affection with the kittens, patting them, singing to them, and generally fussing over them the way we other cat lovers do. Then the kittens were placed in a T-shaped maze where plates of food were concealed and precautions were taken against any olfactory clues. Though Dr. Osis could see the cats, they could not see him.

A series of tests were run with Dr. Osis placing the dishes and it was recorded how many times the cats "guessed" on which side of the T their food was. The amount of correct choices seemed quite a bit higher than mere chance would allow.

To substantiate the suspicion that the cats were receiving clues via ESP from Dr. Osis, an assistant was brought in to run a second series of tests. This assistant had no rapport with the cats and, sure enough, they found the correct side of the T much more infrequently when the assistant ran the test.

Although Osis did not try to separate how much of the psychic communication originated with the experimenter and how much with the cats themselves, his tests were extremely encouraging to those who had been postulating for years that there exists psychic communication between the species.

At the center of American experimentation in the psychic realm has been Dr. J.B. Rhine, long associated with Duke University and subsequently director of a North Carolina-based institute which carried on the work begun at Duke. Rhine was not only concerned with ESP and other psychic phenomena in animals but in the whole unexplored world of so-called extrasensory experience. I say "so-called extrasensory experience" because scientific exploration of psychic animals offers us the hope that much of what we cannot explain—psi-trailing, predictions of death, animals who seem to foretell the future—will one day become more clear to us.

Bill Schul quotes animal researcher Nikko Tinbergen in *The*

Psychic Power of Animals, "If one applies the term (ESP) to perception by process not yet known to us, then extrasensory perception among living creatures may well occur widely. In fact, the echo-location of bats, the function of the lateral line in fishes and the way electric fishes find their prey are all based on processes which we did not know about—and which were thus 'extrasensory' in this sense—only twenty-five years ago."

To be sure, many observable truths about animal behavior seem to favor the psychic explanation. Years ago I heard a story that piqued my interest in the subject. It concerned two horses who had been stable-mates for some time. While one was being ridden in the fields, the other was back in the barn. For some reason, the barn-bound horse came under the discipline of a farm-hand and was struck across the muzzle with a riding crop. At that same time, at least a mile away, the other horse reared as if in sudden pain.

I've had occasion to retell this story, and it is amazing to me how many people have heard accounts wholly similar. Is it ESP or do animal possess super-senses which we have no name for? Observers of wolves have long marveled at the complex system of communication that exists within a pack on the hunt. In pursuit of prey, one wolf seems to know unfailingly and instantly what the others in the pack are going to do. Are they going to surround the prey? Run it into an exhausted state? Is one wolf tiring which will necessitate others to take on his role? All of these messages and others pass effortlessly with the pack at a full-out run.

Or have you ever watched a school of fish and been amazed at the complicated and utterly instantaneous way they can change direction? Their right angle turns are made simultaneously without one fish breaking the pattern. How does each member of the school know the exact instant in which to make the turn? (In the next chapter I'll discuss more fully the psychic world beneath the waters of the world.)

An interesting book about the psychic capacities of animals is called *The Monkey's Tail*, by T.C. Lethbridge. Its author believes that psychic power is a necessary part of all living creatures—

though he feels that in humans psychic power (or psi) is becoming weaker. As for our pets, he says: "Animals have psi-reading and such cats as have been tested mostly have a potential of about 45, as high as *any* human.

"Psi may be related to but is by no means the same as electromagnetism. It doesn't seem to diminish with the square of the distance, as electro-magnetism does. It does not seem to be bound by time or distance in any way that we can see."

Lethbridge points out that our definition of telepathy must be broadened and refined. "We usually think of telepathy," he states "as being the process where a single idea appears to arrive almost simultaneously in the minds of two people. This seems to be a chance happening, and it is often difficult to establish which mind originated the thought. But telepathy is much wider than this and in the case of animals it is clear that individuals of differing species can carry on conversations by its means. In the case of birds, whole flocks operate as one, wheeling and diving with no word of command. Telepathy, in fact, is an alternative method to speech as a means of communication..."

In 1975, Dr. Aristide Esser, a psychiatrist and neurologist, conducted some extremely provocative experiments in Rockland State Hospital in New York. At the conclusion of the experiments, Dr. Esser stated, "There is no doubt in my mind that some dogs, particularly those with a close relationship with their owners, have highly developed ESP."

In one of Dr. Esser's tests, researchers built two copper-lined chambers that were impervious to vibration and soundproof. These soundless rooms were located in different sections of the hospital. "There was no possible way that a subject in one room could have any physical communication with the subject in the other room," stated Dr. Esser. In a representative experiment using these soundproof rooms, the master of two hunting dogs (beagles in this case) was placed inside one of the chambers and given an airgun. Slides of various animals were projected on the wall and the man was instructed to "shoot" these animals. Meanwhile, the two beagles were shut in the other chamber and their responses were monitored through an observation panel. When their master shot at an animal, the dogs went instantaneously wild, barking and whining just as they would on a real hunt. What were they reacting to? They heard nothing, saw nothing. Yet locked in the isolation of the copper-lined room they received a message that sent them into a frenzy.

Another of Dr. Esser's experiments went like this. A pet boxer was hooked up to an electrocardiograph in one soundproof room and its mistress was placed in the other. Without giving the woman any warning, the experimenters sent a man into her room. The man shouted threateningly at her, even hinted he might physically harm her. The woman was definitely scared, and acted it. But what of the dog locked out of sight and with no possibility of hearing? As soon as the woman became scared her boxer's heartbeat registered a violent acceleration.

Dr. Esser also conducted an experiment demonstrating ESP between two animals. This one also involved boxers. A mother boxer and one of her sons were placed in the isolation chambers. Both had been trained to cower at a raised, rolled newspaper. But when someone raised a paper to the son and he cowered, the mother, seeing or hearing none of this, also cowered in her isolated chamber—at the exact same instant! It is no wonder, then, that Dr. Esser says the tests "proved conclusively that some dogs have the power of telepathy."

The problems in the scientific testing of animal psi are at least three-fold. First, of course, is the resistance to the subject within the scientific community. Second, since animal communication seems to be based on senses with which we are now barely acquainted, even those who would like to devise scientific tests are often at a loss to do so. How do you quantify something which you can't see, taste, hear, or touch? How do you measure powers which you yourself lack? Without some pre-existing ideas about what is likely, it is nearly impossible to set up a scientifically approvable experiment. The third major stumbling-block in the scientific study of animal psi is the lack of institutional and governmental support for such tests.

An interesting series of events which demonstrate the problems of ESP research was reported by Jacqueline Himelstein writing in the *National Enquirer*. Himelstein revealed that one of the prime figures in American psi research, J.B. Rhine, had for years been doing secret ESP research for the U.S. Army. The Army (as well as the CIA) has been interested for years in all kinds of paranormal experience. The CIA, for instance, would like to know if ESP can be used for sending secret messages between intelligence agents. In releasing the report covering a full twenty years of secret testing by the Army, the *Enquirer* concentrated on one series of experiments using dogs. "They wanted to find out whether dogs could be used to locate hidden land-mines in military fields by ESP," said Dr. Rhine.

When asked why these tests were kept secret, Rhine was of the opinion that "The popular press in covering this area overemphasizes the sensational aspects of the phenomena rather than discussing it intelligently. So the officials involved in the tests with dogs were probably afraid of strong criticism for having spent money on ESP."

The tests themselves were carried out on a beach north of San Francisco. Small wooden boxes were buried both in the sand and—in order to make certain the dogs couldn't detect any scent—under seawater. The dogs, of course, had no idea where these simulated land-mines were buried and neither did the dogs' handlers. All traces of the burials were scrupulously hidden and even the recorder used to note the dogs' responses remained well out of view.

"The dogs were trained to sit when they discovered a mine," explained Dr. Rhine. "The handler marked the point with an upright stick each time the dog sat, and went on to the next spot. The handler had no ways of knowing whether the dog was correct or not."

The tests were carried out over a period of three months. Two hundred and three tests were run altogether, with five simulated mines being buried for each test. Allowing for the dogs finding the boxes by mere chance, it was decided that a discovery rate of over

20% would be an indication of ESP. (It seems to me that even a 20% discovery rate would be impressive under the circumstances. After all, the testing area was large and the dogs had no clues to work with.) In the first series of tests, the dogs successfully located land mines 51.7% of the time. As is curiously common in the majority of ESP testing situations, the rate of correct choices fell off during the second half of the testing period. (This seems to indicate that as the spontaneity of the tests wears off, the intuitive powers are somewhat lessened by repetition. This situation is somewhat similar to the phenomenon we call "beginner's luck," i.e., our ability to succeed at tasks which we perform without expectations or preconceptions, ability that often trails off when our intellect and/or will-power is brought to bear on the same task. It is "beginner's luck" that can make someone throw a "ringer" the first time they toss a horseshoe and then, when they begin to try in earnest to repeat their success, throw wide of the mark every time thereafter.) Still, with the almost inevitable trailing off of the success rate, the dogs in the land mine experiment scored a success rate of 39.9%—a tenth of a percentage point shy of double the 20% chance rate.

The experiment lent a great deal of credence to the belief that animals possess ESP—or some order of super-sense that we do not yet understand. However, the experiments were soon abandoned, not because of disappointment in the dogs' performance but because the Army couldn't devise a way to find a practical use for ESP. As Dr. Rhine said, "...the man had to lead the dog. Since this was of little use to the Army in practical terms—they wanted dogs that could find the mines without risking men's lives—they gave up the matter."

The Soviet government seems to have pursued researching ESP (in humans as well as animals) without immediate expectation that the results be put to practical use. Though detailed information about animal psi experiments in the Soviet Union remains sketchy and scarce, a fine book is available on the subject. It is called *Psychic Discoveries Behind the Iron Curtain*. In the '60s, Americans learned that the University of Leningrad had a special laboratory for the study of telepathy run by the Department of Physiology under the direction of Professor L.L. Vasiliev. Vasiliev dates the Soviet interest in animal psi back to the '20s. It began at the University of Leningrad with a work done by a researcher named Bechterev, a renowned brain physiologist. Bechterev traced his fascination with psychic animals to the observation that many dogs who performed in the circus responded to their trainers' commands before the commands were given or before any signal whatsoever had been transmitted. Bechterev ran a long series of experiments with trained dogs, using traditional scientific methods, and came to the conclusion that there was definitely a psychic power in these dogs that allowed them to learn the commands through precognition.

In France and the Netherlands, very elaborate, sophisticated experiments were run to test the level of precognition in those stand-by laboratory animals—mice. The French tests were supervised by a Professor Duval. They built a contraption which gave off random (and slight) electric shocks. The electrified box was divided down the middle and the mice had no way of knowing which side would give the shock. (The experimenters didn't control this either; the electricity was controlled by a random number generator.) Though the mice certainly suffered their share of shocks, an unusually high number of instances saw them uncannily choose the safe side of the box, in a sequence and number that far exceeded random behavior. The conclusion drawn by the French was that the mice were definitely making their choices based on a higher, unknown sense—a sense which the scientists themselves called ESP.

A few years later, a follow-up to Duval's experiment was designed by Sybo A. Schouten, a Dutch scientist. Rather than using a negative stimulus, Schouten trained mice to respond to a reward—in this case, a drop of drinking water.

Again, the results were very convincingly on the side of ESP and clairvoyance. Mice were placed in separate cages in separate rooms. Each set of mice was given only half the clue needed to choose the response which would bring the reward. In order to get the water, the mice needed to see a flashing light which would direct them to the correct lever to push. But the mice in the cage with the lever had no light, and those with the light had no lever. Over a period of time, it became statistically proven that the mice that saw the light transmitted this information to the mice in the cage with the lever, enabling these mice to release the drop of water for both sets of mice.

In order to be sure that the lightless mice weren't just extraordinarily lucky, the test was also run without the second set of mice seeing the light clue. In those cases, the number of correct responses fell markedly. The Dutch scientists concluded that the mice who saw the light communicated this information to their counterparts in the other cage—though how this information was communicated remained an unanswered question.

Most of the laboratory work with psychic animals ends with unanswered questions. It is unclear how much of the mystery of silent communication will be unraveled in the scientific laboratory. What remains clear, however, is that the systematic and controlled study of psychic animals is, as yet, in its infancy. Experiments are modest and infrequent. There are no multi-million dollar grants on the horizon for the study of animal psi.

J.B. Rhine has collected hundreds of stories of psi-trailing, some of which can be found in the chapter called "The Cosmic Compass," but even Rhine's work remains inconclusive. What is encouraging, however, for those of us who yearn to know more about what animals can teach us about the mind, is that all of the experiments have yielded positive results. Whether the scientific community will pursue these positive results and begin a study of psychic animals on a large-scale basis is a question that waits to be answered.

THIRTEEN

Psychics of the Deep: Dolphins, Orcas, and Others

The dolphin has always been a source of fascination and comfort to humans. The earliest sailors saw dolphins as good omens, and their playfulness has delighted men and women from earliest times. There is probably no other creature more genuinely gentle, witty, affectionate, and playful than this sea-going mammal. One of the family of mammals (the cetaceans) who, after leaving the sea to evolve on land, returned to life in the water, the dolphin has a unique place in the scheme of things. Probably no other animal—with the possible exception of the chimpanzee—offers as much hope in bridging the gap between human and animal consciousness.

The family of cetaceans include the dolphin, porpoise, whale and orca. While it is generally believed that our closest physical look-alikes in the animal kingdom can be found in the simian family, it is acknowledged now that the intelligence of the dolphin most resembles human intelligence. While it is clear that they are like us in terms of culture, group life, predilection toward speech, culture, playfulness, sense of humor, and even morality, it is only in very recent years that any concerted attempt has been made to communicate with dolphins. Part of the reason is that their home in the sea made them less accessible to us than monkeys and gorillas and, of course, much less casually observable.

Our fascination with monkeys has been in part based on our striking physical resemblance, whereas dolphins have neither hands nor feet. (Interestingly enough, it is now known that at a certain stage of embryonic development the white-sided dolphin bears a very striking resemblance to the human fetus. The neck is constricted, the head is dome-shaped and perpendicular to the spine, the nose is located in the facial area, and the beginnings of limbs and ears are also evident.)

Anyone who has ever encountered a dolphin seems to experience an almost startling sense of affection and penetration of mind. Dolphins rarely fail to astound humans—they are well-known as gracious hosts, tireless entertainers (in captivity as well as on the open sea) and unhesitating heroes in time of peril.

But two of their best known and most important qualities are those of extremely high intelligence and powerful psychic ability. As Carl Sagan, the noted astronomer and author of *The Dragons of Eden*, said, referring to the cetacean family, "There is at least moderately convincing evidence that there is another class of intelligent beings on earth besides ourselves."

In June of 1976, another of many dolphin stories appeared in the *National Enquirer*. This story involved a 12-foot, 650-lb. dolphin named Beaky, who was well known to the local divers in Mount's Bay, near Cornwall, England. Beaky was known as a rascal, full of curiosity, mischief and general playfulness toward divers. That is until he became a hero.

Keith Monery, a 24-year-old diving student, was in peril: his life-jacket began to leak and he could no longer keep himself above water. He was being weighted down by the equipment he had strapped to his back and he began to panic. He thrashed about to give the other divers his distress signal (a clenched fist waved from side to side). The signal was seen by Bob and Hazel Carswell, the diving instructors, and they responded immediately. Hazel dove into the water. As she swam toward the drowning Keith she felt something large shoot past her beneath the water: it was Beaky.

Beaky reached Keith long before Hazel, and began to nudge

Keith upward toward the surface and kept him afloat for several minutes before Hazel could reach him. When she finally did reach him Beaky continued to nudge them afloat and lightly push them toward the safety of the craft where Bob waited.

How did Beaky know that this man was in danger? And further, how did Beaky know exactly how to deal with the problem? Intelligence doesn't explain very much of Beaky's efforts—it is much more. Beaky had to read the thoughts of the student in peril— he had to receive quite a few clear messages: what was wrong; what needed to be done; how to do it; and exactly how to carry it out to the finish.

This takes high intelligence but what must be considered is how Beaky received these messages, what language came into play. It was the silent language, the instinct of communication through the universal sixth sense. Because Beaky is a creature who constantly uses his psychic abilities, he was able to read and understand exactly those communication signals sent out by Keith.

Again, a reporter from the Associated Press stationed in Moscow sent news of an amazing occurrence on October 18, 1967, recorded Schul in his book. A group of dolphins requested assistance from a fishing boat in the Black Sea. The group of dolphins began to swim around the fishing boat, finally surrounding it and began to maneuver it off course toward a buoy nearby. When the fishermen saw that a young dolphin was trapped in the anchorline they realized that the dolphins needed human hands to manipulate the rope. They set to work, freeing the baby dolphin. The fishermen succeeded in no time, and the dolphin troop let out high-pitched joyous whistles of gratitude and leaped about the boat. They even escorted the fishing vessel back to port.

Dolphins and people of the sea come to know each other well after much meeting in their fishing districts. These fishermen knew one certain fact about any encounter with a dolphin: that they would under no circumstances harm a human being. While the major threat to the cetacean world is the careless and brutal attacks committed by humans on dolphins (from drowning dolphins in tuna-fishing nets to the slaughter of countless whales, almost to the point of extinction).

Schul reports in his book that V. Droescher, a nature writer, states "...not a single case has ever been recorded of a dolphin's making a hostile gesture toward a man—not even when that man is engaged in killing the dolphin." This concurs with the research I have done, though I've found no logical reason for it. Are the dolphins just gentle beings or is it something else? We know that dolphins can be fierce fighters, as in battle with sharks or killer whales. Why is their treatment of humans so forgiving and trusting? One hopes we will know in the near future if what some propose comes true: that it is more likely that our first complex conversations with non-humans will be with dolphins, barring possible contact with intelligence from Outer Space.

Arthur C. Clarke, the science writer, has suggested that, as dolphins have no written language or records, there is good reason to believe that an oral history is passed down from generation to generation, probably from mother to baby. The nursing period for mother and baby is between 18 to 21 months and they are extremely close during this period John C. Lilly, the famous naturalist and dolphin expert, has often speculated whether the mother teaches her baby everything that the baby will need to know for the rest of its life concerning dolphin culture, legends and conceptual knowledge.

For the sake of clarity, let's look at the fascinating evolution of the physical biology that has taken place in the cetacean world.

It is through the work of Sterling Bunnell, a psychiatrist and evolutionary ecologist, that we take a look at the startling facts about the evolution of the cetacean brain and intelligence.

Tooth structure and nose placement of early fossils indicate strongly that whales evolved from a carnivorous mammal that roamed the African shores. These fossils also show that fifty million years ago the whale had already adapted itself to aquatic life. Ten million years later, the skull had begun to telescope and the nostrils moved behind or above the eyes. Our modern dolphin began to appear about twenty-five million years ago. What is most important to note here is that in the cetacean groups skull telescoping (which includes the backward movement of the nostrils) was accompanied by an increase in brain size. The South American river dolphin had the brain size of a human thirty million years ago. So in contrast to our recent evolution as thinking humans (one million years) whales had developed their brain size earlier and more gradually.

One of the fascinating things about the cetacean family is that their brains continued to increase in size without there being any direct physical or environmental necessity for this increase. Students of dolphins, whales, and other cetaceans now tell us that the most likely reasons for this increase in brain size are social and sexual. In other words, the brain has enlarged because of he cultural and psychological content of cetacean life. If all cetaceans needed was to navigate the sea and find food, the complexity of their brains would be completely superfluous. But the fact is that dolphins and other mammals have developed capacities that give them detailed and instantaneous information about matters that go far beyond information needed solely for survival. Echolocation, for example, not only assists the dolphin in navigating the seas but gives a three-dimensional detailed understanding of the emotional and physical state of other dolphins.

Most of the increased brain size in cetaceans has come in the area of the cerebral cortex which is an area of the brain used for general association and senses of cultural hierarchy. In other words, brain size has increased with the growing complexities and refinement of cetacean social life. The survival mechanisms of the cetacean seem to have reached their full development thousands of years ago and all subsequent development has been in the area of finer modes of interspecies communication.

Each species' brain is constructed uniquely; the fascinating thing is the ways in which they are different. That part of the brain that is related to intellectual acuity and the many facets of perception is considered by scientists in the field to be as developed in the dolphin as in the human, though arranged differently. The areas of the brain concerned with receiving information from face and ears are large, while the area concerned with motor control takes up less space than in the human brain. This is clearly because cetaceans are concerned mainly with swimming and vocalizing. It is these simple facts that led Bunnell to believe that the orientation of the cetacean mind is toward perception and interpersonal relations. The human mind is more oriented toward communication through physical movement and through the use of the hands.

That part of the brain called the neocortex is the part that forms thoughts, perceptions and memories. Its motivation source is the activity of the limbic system, or core brain. Much research data collected from investigation of brain damage in humans points to the importance of a high ratio of neocortical association neurons to limbic system brain-stem neurons in order for, as Bunnell states, "qualities as reality orientation, objectivity, humor, emotional self-control, and the capacity for logically consistent abstract thought, as well as the higher forms of creativity." When the ratio of those particular neurons is decreased the effect is the opposite of the above. Dolphins, according to Bunnell, have a higher neocortical-limbic ratio than most intelligent humans.

There is a part of the dolphin brain not found in any other mammal. It is called the paralimbic lobe and its function is the integration of all sensory and motor areas represented together. In humans, these sensory areas are widely separated and so it takes longer for perceptual information to be digested. It is the cetacean's paralimbic lobe which fosters the rapid formation of related perceptions.

To put it more plainly, through the echolocation and forehead reflector for the sound production system, vocalization in the cetacean world has many facets to it. It is not only used as language but as an X-ray and radar system all in one. When a dolphin vocalizes at certain pitches, those vocalizations are bounced off their target to convey important information to include a perceptual image of every aspect of that dolphin, including its inner biological functioning.

It is their echolocation system which supplies them with such detailed images of objects. There is strong evidence that the dolphin recreates the very sounds of a particular perception in order to communicate not only particular data but to recreate and project an image to the receiving dolphin.

The implications of all of these facts and speculations concerning cetacean intelligence and culture are wide-ranging. One can see immediately that with such a complex and developed form of communication, the psychic realm would be as integrated a part as the rest. There is no limit to what we may learn about the universal language through these aquatic mammals.

I, along with many others, believe that when we finally have a two-way communication with cetaceans, our own perception of the world, the universe's workings will be utterly changed; the basis of all of our cultural assumptions and beliefs will either be shaken to the core, or reenforced with new and startling information.

But more than that, communication with cetaceans would most assuredly mean a greater knowledge of their everyday tool: ESP or psychic energy.

This brings us to the man who has done most to further us on our way toward communicating with the dolphin; Dr. John Lilly.

Dr. Lilly is best known for his dedication and success in the study of the dolphin. His (and his dolphins') most profound accomplishment is in the very beginnings of possible communication between the species.

The first spark came in 1957 when Dr. Lilly obtained a mimicry effect by use of electrodes implanted in the rewarding points of a dolphin's brain.

But it was in 1960 that a dolphin named Lizzie, at Dr. Lilly's laboratory in St. Thomas, produced sounds that were strikingly similar to human noises. Lizzie and another dolphin, Baby, lived in the same pool and exclusively communicated in 'dolphinese.' It was the night before Lizzie died that, alone in her tank, for the first time, she spoke underwater: she said, "It's six o'clock." These are the exact words that Dr. Lilly had just shouted to her above water. Dr. Lilly and his co-worker Miss Miller studied the tape and felt surely that Lizzie had in fact said the above.

It was the dolphin Elvar who truly astonished Dr. Lilly. Elvar came to the lab after Lizzie died and within a year had begun to experiment with strange new vocalizations. His usual 'dolphinese' was mingled with quacking, buzzing, barks, wails and most interesting of all, banjo-like sounds. Mostly he made these sounds underwater but soon he began to make them above water. They began to vaguely resemble human speech.

There began an intensive effort to make Elvar vocalize or mimic human speech. One of the most notable moments of this long experiment was when Miss Miller was again in a session with Elvar. Miss Miller began saying, "More, Elvar," and Elvar came back with, "More, Var," at once slowing up his natural vocalizing pace and then speeding it up. He then said the complete, "More, Elvar," and did the same slowing and speeding of it. It must be remembered here that dolphins often vocalize at an intensely high volume and pitch so that when Elvar slowed down his vocalization and lowered his pitch it could resemble human sounds.

Most exciting of all is the story of Chee-Chee who lived in the adjacent tank to Elvar. Chee-Chee was never asked to produce sounds. The two dolphins were friends and on weekends were allowed to spend much time together for courtship and companionship, and it seems that during their visits Elvar had been giving Chee-Chee some lessons in speaking. When it came time for Chee-Chee to begin her turn at human vocalizing she responded well on the first try. It was noticed at that point that Elvar and Chee-Chee were interspersing human sounds (above water) in their communication. Chee-Chee therefore was able to produce human sounds on the first try with her human instructor.

The truly amazing thing is that it was the dolphins, really, who stepped forward to break the communication barrier, not the humans. As Dr. Lilly has said, we have not been able to break down the hieroglyphics of 'dolphinese.' What Dr. Lilly did do though was to communicate, through the silent language, what he wanted the dolphins to do and they responded in the best ways they could, through a cultural barrier of at least a million years.

It is the human's greatest wish to communicate with all things, our wish to know everything, but mainly to know the truth. Strangely enough we have concentrated on the simplest form of communication: that of physical vocalization.

The time to step forward is, quite clearly and urgently, now. Lilly's experiments with dolphin speech as well as the remarkable (and very well publicized) experiments with "talking chimpanzees" taking place in primate labs, give us reason to believe that the gaps which separate human from animal will soon disappear. We will have in the not too distant future a class of speaking animals. From these remarkable trained animals we are certain to learn amazing things about animal social life and animal perception. As thrilling as this prospect is, it is, quite clearly, a limited one. We are concentrating only on teaching animals to speak in our language—the language of nouns and verbs. But the most profound understanding of both animal and human nature will come when we also learn to concentrate on animal language—the language of gesture, empathy, and telepathy. It is in the silent language that the most crucial and deepest secrets of the animal mind are held.

Psychic Pets and the
New Human Consciousness

I n the United States about eight per cent of the people live in
cities. Urban lifestyles mean that more and more people must
learn to live in less and less space. Our cities are filled with massive
apartment complexes where vertical living arrangements allow
thousands of people to live where, half a century earlier, only one
family lived. As urban life becomes more widespread and more
complex, there are, from time to time, people who come forward
and warn us that if we do not return to earlier, simpler ways of life
we are doomed. To be sure, every year a certain small number of
people trickle out of the cities and attempt to "return" to rural or
smalltown life. Some observers, hungry perhaps for a trend to write
about, find in those isolated instances a reason to believe that
America as a whole is becoming less urban, less technological. But
simple statistics say otherwise, and we must accept the fact that, for
this stage of our development, *homo sapiens* is an urban creature,
one who rarely sees trees or open spaces, whose modes of
locomotion are almost entirely mechanical, and whose systems of
information gathering are primarily electronic.

This is not, of course, a distinctly American phenomenon. Even
out-of-the-way island resorts now feature gleaming white hotels
and in farmlands the gigantic TV antenna, built to pull in signals

from the distant city, looms as mightily as the windmill once did. All of Europe and now Africa and Asia is grouping into complex urban environments where the sophistication of commerce and industry sets the mood for daily life.

As we become more and more settled (or resigned) in our modern lifestyles we seem to feel deeper yearnings for our pasts. Marshall McLuhan would have it that it is human nature to speed into the future while peering into the rearview mirror. But even if nostalgia is merely an instinctual reaction to what author Alvin Toffler refers to as "future shock," the fact is that modern life awakens in humans a need to better know their past, to touch their origins before the momentum of their daily life takes them too far away. These past few years have witnessed a burgeoning interest in ancestral origins.

Families separated from their forebears by centuries and oceans are consumed with a desire to know their *origins* which borders on obsession. Once the idea of a "family tree" was the province of the rich—it was a way of boasting of prominent ancestors and, much worse, boasting of some bogus pedigree. But today, family trees are no longer the stuff of coats-of-arms and full page write-ups in *Who's Who*.

Today, people from all strata of life long to learn about their ancestors and are willing to embrace great-grandfathers and distant cousins, be they peddlers, slaves, midwives, parsons, or riverboat captains. The point in tracing family genealogy is no longer to discover illustrious ancestors but to make contact with the past—to make one's own life more real by tracing one's antecedents.

What does all of this have to do with our pets? A great deal, I think. I have lived with dogs and cats in the city and I have lived with all kinds of pets in the country and nothing I know of can put me more "in touch" with myself than trying to understand (and make myself understood by) an animal.

For all the nostalgia we might feel for a way of life simpler and more peaceful than the one we know, our real longing, I think, is to know ourselves as we really are. Sometimes our dissatisfaction with modern times is based on the feeling that the complexity, the technology, the uncertainty, and the plasticity all serve to separate us from our true and elemental selves.

Some of the truth of our essential nature may be found in discovering our ancestral roots—but why stop just a few generations into the past? The relatives we may discover in Ireland or Iran can only populate our recent past—and besides, they are essentially vanished. They exist only in photographs, in old yellowed letters, in stories passed from generation to generation. The wisdom they bring to us is vague, obscured by time, second-hand, and as often as not utterly puzzling.

If you are interested in touching your inner self, then why not look to relatives who are both incredibly distant and totally alive? I'm speaking, of course, of the cats, dogs, birds, horses, and other pets with whom we can share our daily lives. You may not be able to swap stories about Great Grandma's marble cake with your Airedale. But a loving and understanding of an animal will, if you let it, take you deeper into a sense of your origins than a hundred genealogical charts.

I have tried to convey my sense of what we can learn from animals. The more I have observed and the more I have considered the evidence, the more certain I've become that the animals in our midst offer us a unique and crucial opportunity. Consider: often, out of our desire to know and experience the past, we have fantasied a "time machine," a contraption which would penetrate the time dimension, turn back the clock, and allow us to live in the past and see it as it actually was. Impatient with the bloodlessness of historical records, as frustrated as they were illuminated by archaelogical findings, forced to guess and surmise about the true nature of the past, historians and antiquarians have always yearned for a way to make the past more real, to somehow enter it.

But the amazing fact is that a crucial part of our past is alive and well, and living with us at this instant. The past, I might say, is curled peacefully at my feet as I type these very words. Specifically,

I'm talking about my yellow cat, and, in general, I refer to all of the millions of animals with whom we humans share our lives.

The number of pet owners has, over the past decade, increased at a fantastic, unprecedented rate. A trip to a New York City public park is like a visit to a Dogs of the World show—Afghans, Borzois, Poodles, Chows, and hundreds of other breeds and mixtures meet daily, to greet and test one another, to perform elaborate social rituals, to share the canine sense of life. Off to the side, you will find the dog owners, holding the unfastened leads and smiling, eyeing their dogs with the nervousness of a new parent.

Likewise in big cities, the number of household cats has increased—cat foods and accessories are a major American business. An orange tabby cat called Morris who has been used to advertise a brand of cat food became almost overnight a national celebrity. Morris even "wrote" a book, which promptly became a best seller, and his death in the summer of 1978 was mourned by millions. At the same time, city dwellers also developed a mania for keeping house plants. It was sometime after the millionth jade plant was sold that people began saying that plants were not insensate but had feelings, responded to classical music, and were capable of telepathy.

Some say that our current obsession with cats and dogs and birds and plants is a result of the loneliness and isolation of much of city life. In an environment where it is difficult to trust your neighbors, the unquestioning loyalty of a dog can be a comfort. In an environment filled with noise and ugliness, the unfailing silent grace of a cat can satisfy the yearning for peace and order. As more and more families dissolve, as more and more old people must live their final years alone, the presence of a beloved pet can lessen the often terrifying solitude.

But is it just these things that have more and more people seeking the company of animals? I think not.

We are, at this time, in a uniquely promising point in the history of the relationship between humans and animals. The fight between organized religion and paganism has long since exhausted itself. There is no longer a strident official policy warning us against magicians, of wizards and their hellish hounds, of witches and their evil feline assistants. No longer do the representatives need to rail against the animal gods or the half human-half animal deities. Likewise, the Puritan grip on the Western imagination has been well loosened over the course of the twentieth century. If once animal nature represented all of the forbidden sexuality which our ancestors lived with and denied, our fear of sexuality has slowly lessened until now we are, more than ever before, ready not only to accept our animal nature but also to increase it. While once men and women prayed to be *more* civilized, *more* restrained, today the quest is quite the opposite: we long to be more free, more natural and spontaneous.

The subsiding of religious rivalries and the gradual acceptance of sexuality have combined to make us, both consciously and unconsciously, more receptive to the glories of animal nature. Now, more than any other time since the ebb of the ancient world, men and women not only can keep animals but also learn to identify with them—to appreciate the uniqueness of animal perceptions, the astonishing power of animal super-senses, and the complexity of animal social organization.

It is in this growing identification with our pets that we can find one of the most profound opportunities of our lives. I am speaking of nothing less the the recapture of our intuitive capacity. To all of those who know there is more to owning a dog than teaching him how to bark at strangers, and more to living with a cat than teaching him not to scratch the furniture, life with a beloved pet offers a glimpse at a perceptual paradise.

Our pets can, when we let them, teach us to use our intuition as well as our psychic power in a way that many of us never thought possible. That's why when people tell me about all of the things they've taught their pets I like to say, "Sometimes it's easier to teach than to learn. Tell me about what your pet has taught *you.*"

If the answer to that question is "Nothing," then the pleasure and, yes, the *awakening* of living with an animal is being passed by in favor of the conventional master-slave relationship most people establish with their pets. There is no doubt but that some animals are more psychic than others. But there is hardly an animal in existence who cannot, in one way or another, teach us a great deal about listening to and speaking the silent language of universal consciousness.

Our pets are in our homes. They are with us at this moment. Now it is up to us: *listen*.